THE **MINI** ROUGH GUIDE TO
MALLORCA

T0321232

ROUGH
GUIDES

YOUR TAILOR-MADE TRIP
STARTS HERE

Tailor-made trips and unique adventures crafted by local experts

Rough Guides has been inspiring travellers for more than 35 years. Leave it to our local experts to create your perfect itinerary and book it at local rates.

Don't follow the crowd – find your own path.

HOW ROUGHGUIDES.COM/TRIPS WORKS

STEP 1 Pick your dream destination, tell us what you want and submit an enquiry.

STEP 2 Fill in a short form to tell your local expert about your dream trip and preferences.

STEP 3 Our local expert will craft your tailor-made itinerary. You'll be able to tweak and refine it until you're completely satisfied.

STEP 4 Book online with ease, pack your bags and enjoy the trip! Our local expert will be on hand 24/7 while you're on the road.

PLAN AND BOOK YOUR TRIP AT
ROUGHGUIDES.COM/TRIPS

HOW TO DOWNLOAD YOUR FREE EBOOK

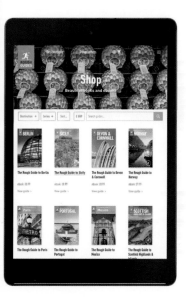

1. Visit **www.roughguides.com/free-ebook** or scan the **QR code** below

2. Enter the code **mallorca295**

3. Follow the simple step-by-step instructions

For troubleshooting contact: mail@roughguides.com

10 THINGS NOT TO MISS

A PERFECT DAY

9am

Breakfast. Kick off the day in Palma with breakfast at the trendy *Mise En Place* in Plaça Major, where a delicious array of treats – home-made pastries, fresh fruit, coffee – awaits you. It's slightly hidden, but well worth seeking out.

10am

In search of Chopin. Take the road that runs about 10km (6 miles) through olive and almond groves to Valldemossa, where La Real Cartuja holds the apartment in which George Sand and Frédéric Chopin once stayed. In Palau del Rei Sancho next doot, recitals of Chopin's music are held throughout the day.

Noon

Sweet treat. Linger over coffee and a *coca de patata*, a sweet local pastry, in the Carrer Blanquera.

1pm

Delightful Deià. Continue on the scenic coast road to Deià, a dinky, honey-coloured town that was home to poet Robert Graves and still attracts writers and artists. Meander through the picturesque streets and browse in the boutiques.

2pm

Graves's grave. Break for tapas in *El Barrigon Xelini* (see page 109), a huge, atmospheric bar with tables spilling outside onto a pleasant terrace. Afterwards, follow the literary trail and visit the poet's simple grave in the hilltop cemetery, before swinging by his home, Ca N'Alluny, which has been reimagined as a small museum.

IN **MALLORCA**

3.30pm

Sea swims. Strike out on the 35-minute walk through olive and lemon groves to the Cala Deià, a pretty little rocky cove where you can swim in crystalline waters.

4.30pm

Sóller. From Deià, drive the scenic coast road, flanked by orchards of citrus trees and gnarled olive groves, for half an hour until you dip into the broad valley of Sóller. Park up to explore the bustling little town itself, lined with well-preserved eighteenth- and nineteenth-century mansions. Pause for an espresso in the café-lined square, Plaça Sa Constitució, while admiring the *Moderniste* architecture and soaking up everyday local life.

6pm

Spectacular sunset. Wend your way back down the coast to Son Marroig, home to a nineteenth-century Austrian archduke who fell in love with the island. You can visit his house and gardens, but the main attraction is watching the sunset over Na Foradada.

8pm

Dinner. Take your pick from one of Deià's many excellent restaurants. Go upmarket with the modern menu at *El Olivo* (part of *Belmond La Residencia* hotel), or indulge in lobster with asparagus ravioli at *Sebastian* (see page 110).

11pm

Nightlife. Back in Palma, take a scenic stroll along the harbour, then perhaps end the night with a cocktail or two at *Abaco* (see page 94) in the old town.

CONTENTS

A NOTE TO READERS

At Rough Guides, we always strive to bring you the most up-to-date information. This book was produced during a period of continuing uncertainty caused by the Covid-19 pandemic, so please note that content is more subject to change than usual. We recommend checking the latest restrictions and official guidance.

OVERVIEW

Mallorca could claim to be the perfect holiday island, blessed with attributes that entice millions of foreign visitors annually. The deep blue and translucent turquoise of the Mediterranean, hundreds of kilometres of coastline, secluded rocky coves and wide sandy beaches, a vibrant and sophisticated capital city and some 300 days of brilliant sunshine each year make it irresistible.

A VARIED LANDSCAPE

Lying off the northeast coast of Spain, Mallorca is the largest of the five Balearic Islands, but it is not a big place. It has more than 550km (325 miles) of coastline, but at its widest point – Cap de Sa Mola in the southwest to Capdepera in the northeast – it is only 100km (60 miles) across; at its narrowest, from the Badia d'Alcúdia in the north to the Badia de Palma in the south, it's only claws half that distance.

The landscape, however, is extremely varied. The dramatic cliffs edging the Serra de Tramuntana, a World Heritage Site, hug the west coast from Andratx all the way to Cap de Formentor. The coastal scenery is stunning, with dizzying drops to the sea and the tiny coves far below, and picturesque villages set among centuries-old terraces. To the northwest, away from the coast, the Tramuntana range provides ideal walking and climbing conditions. There

> ### Blue Flag beaches
>
> Mallorca's beaches didn't always have the sterling reputation they do today. Following a major clean-up campaign, 31 of the 46 Blue Flag beaches in the Balearic Islands belong to Mallorca, a testament to their safety and cleanliness.

Views along the west coast

are 10 main peaks, the highest of which is Puig Major at 1,445 metres (4,741ft). The north coast is dominated by the Bay of Alcúdia – 12km (8 miles) of fine golden sand sloping into shallow waters – and by the grassy wetlands of S'Albufera, now a protected natural park. The interior is a large plain with sleepy towns, sandstone churches, well-tended farmland, groves of ancient olive trees and orchards of almonds and apricots. On the east coast, long sweeps of beach alternate with intimate little coves and spectacular cave formations, while several picturesque fishing harbours retain their individuality. The south centres on the cosmopolitan capital, Palma, and its splendid bay. Around it, to the east and west, unfurl the crowded beaches whose glorious sands first brought mass tourism to the island in the late 1950s.

CLIMATE

Mallorca's climate is heavenly for northern Europeans. Although summer extremes of 34°C (93°F) can be uncomfortable, the July–August average is a balmy 24°C (76°F); winters are mild and not too wet, and even the timid can swim in the sea from June to October.

VEGETATION AND BIRDLIFE

The flora of the island is as diverse as the landscape. There are cultivated olives, almonds, apricot and citrus trees; holm oaks and pines flourish in mountainous regions, with rosemary, lavender and heather turning the hillsides purple. Sturdy palm trees grow at sea level, and bougainvillaea brightens village walls; while wild orchids and water-loving reeds, sedges and poplars thrive in the S'Albufera marshes.

Mallorca is rich in birdlife. Come in spring, as so many bird-watchers do, to glimpse the numerous migratory species that set up temporary home here. The Boquer Valley, near Pollença, is popular with those in the know. S'Albufera, on the north coast, plays host to numerous resident and migrant species, including the cattle egrets that can be seen perched on the backs of cows, pecking insects from their hides, and birds such as Eleonora's falcons, which typically arrive in late spring and hang around until late October to early November. Among the most colourful and exotic birds that can be seen in many locations in summer are bee-eaters and hoopoes. The island of Cabrera and the Parc Natural de Mondragó in the southeast corner are among the best places to spot migrating seabirds.

THE ISLANDERS AND THEIR LANGUAGE

The population of Mallorca is approximately 895,000, of whom a little less than half – 405,000 – live in the capital. The rest are scattered across 53 municipal districts, with the interior plain – Es Pla – being the most sparsely populated region. In the peak summer season, tourists – some fourteen million a year, some sixty percent of whom are German or English – and hordes of seasonal workers, many from Andalusia, swell the population and strain the infrastructure and water supply to their limits.

Mallorcans are bilingual in Spanish and in Mallorquín, a variant of Catalan, which is the official language. Most signs and street names are written in Catalan, and this is the language people choose to speak among themselves, and which is

Magaluf was among the first of the large-scale resorts

used in schools. However, visitors will find locals quite happy to address them in Castilian Spanish, and the high number of seasonal workers from the mainland ensures that Spanish is spoken everywhere.

TOURISM TRENDS

Mallorca was one of the first places in Spain to be developed for tourism in the 1950s. Ever since, it has been one of the major centres, and tourism is now responsible for nearly 90 percent of the island's income. But the industry has had contradictory effects. Income from it made this region Spain's wealthiest per capita, but the environment effects of being Europe's low-budget playground have taken a heavy toll. Four decades after the initital explosion, tourism overheated, leaving a forest of towering hotels and beach-hugging villa communities, whole resorts lined with fast-food outlets, tourist tat shops, and loud clubs and bars serving ludicrously cheap alcohol. This has led local residents to seek ways to limit so-called 'bad tourist activity', including changing how free alcohol is served at all-inclusive resorts and increasing the Sustainable Tourist Tax.

In the 1990s, the island government realized it was time to reassess Mallorca's tourism industry. Fearing that massive overdevelopment and the increasingly bad reputation earned by the raucous behaviour of some visitors, as well as new trends in international tourism, were leaving the Balearics behind, the authorities took action. Moves were made to protect the remaining undeveloped areas as nature preserves, proclaiming them off-limits to construction, and demolishing some of the more unsightly hotel complexes. Almost one-third of the island is now under some kind of protection order, and the advantages to the landscape and wildlife are palpable.

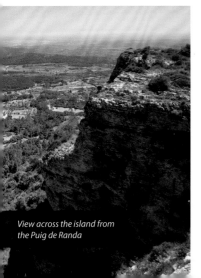

There have also been energetic moves to encourage a more upmarket and environmentally friendly kind of tourism. The government's *agroturisme* initiative, which promotes accommodation in small rural hotels and *fincas* (farmhouses) has been extremely popular, both with visitors looking for peace and quiet amid scenic surroundings, and farming families who were struggling to keep their properties going.

View across the island from the Puig de Randa

Walking paths have been opened up and clearly marked, and a number of hilltop sanctuaries provide rest and respite for hikers; natural parks are widely promoted and user-friendly. Considerable investment has gone into golf courses and marinas to attract higher-income tourists, and luxury resort and boutique hotels are springing up across the island.

In Palma de Mallorca, guided walking tours encourage visitors to appreciate the city's heritage, while the range and calibre of the capital's museums and cultural centres is impressive.

ENJOYING THE ISLAND

Throughout the island, summer music festivals are held in beautiful historic buildings, attracting internationally known performers, while traditional, local festivals are also being promoted as a way of disseminating the rural culture of the Balearics. There has also been a renewed interest in Mallorcan food, *cuina Mallorquina*, and many venues, from the traditional *cellers* (see page 72) to gourmet restaurants and more basic haunts are experiencing a surge in popularity.

Mallorca is easy to get around. Hiring a car is relatively inexpensive, but far from stress-free: many roads (especially the stretch around the Bay of Palma) get very busy, especially in summer, and parking almost everywhere is a major pain. Public transport, however, is excellent: there are regular buses from Palma to most points of interest (some services are limited on Sundays), and regular rail service – including the scenic rail journey on the narrow-gauge line between Palma and Sóller (see page 53). For another aspect of the island, you can take boat trips along much of the coast.

With all of this going for it, Mallorca is much more than simply a place for sun, sea and sand, though this holiday holy grail still rules the local roost.

HISTORY AND CULTURE

Many influences have shaped Mallorca over the past 4000 years and helped make it the fascinating place it is today. The stone towers called *talayots* that can still be seen in parts of the island were defensive structures built by early inhabitants, who are believed to have made settlements here around 1300BC. Even before that, Neolithic islanders had graduated from cave dwellings to simple stone houses, and cleared fields by piling stones into dividing walls – the origins of the intricate dry-stone walls called *parets seques* or *margers* that can still be seen in the island interior.

Over the centuries, the inhabitants traded with the Phoenicians, Carthaginians and Greeks, and the Carthaginians gradually colonized the islands (c. 400BC), absorbed them into their trading empire and founded the main ports. But by 123BC, the Romans, who had pacified most of Spain at this point, despatched an invading force to conquer the islands, which they named Balearis Major (Mallorca) and Balearis Minor (Menorca).

Balearic slingers

The early inhabitants' skill with stones was evident in their deadly use of the slingshot. The 'Balearic slingers' were renowned throughout the Mediterranean world and recruited by Hannibal to fight for the Carthaginians in the Punic Wars against Rome. The name Balearic probably comes from the Greek word, *ballein*, 'to throw'.

ROMANS, VANDALS AND MOORISH OCCUPATION

The Romans introduced the Christianity, constructed roads and established the towns of Palmaria (Palma) and Pollentia (near Alcúdia), but during the fifth century AD, as the Roman Empire crumbled, Goths, Vandals and Visigoths poured into the Balearics. The Vandals destroyed almost all evidence of Roman occupation – the remains of Pollentia outside Alcúdia are among the very few traces left – before they were ousted in 533AD by a Byzantine expedition from Constantinople.

But more invaders were to follow. Ignited by the teachings of the Prophet Mohammed, Islam spread quickly in the eighth century. A Moorish army led by General Tarik landed on the Iberian Peninsula in 711 and, in just seven years, most of Spain was under Moorish rule. While the Balearics remained submissive, the *caliphs* (rulers) were content to accept tribute from them, but local disturbances prompted an invasion at the beginning of the tenth century. Both islands were conquered and became part of the Caliphate of Córdoba.

The talayotic settlement at Ses Païsses

Although little Moorish architecture remains – the Arab Baths in Palma and the Jardins d'Alfàbia near Sóller are two exceptions – the influence can be seen in Palma, in the Palau de l'Almudaina, in the fountains in S'Hort del Rei, and in many shady patios. Some place names are also of Arabic origin – Alcúdia (Al-Kudia) means 'on the hill', and Binissalem means 'son of peace'.

THE RECONQUEST

The aim of the crusades in Spain was the eviction of the Muslims or Moors – a process called the *Reconquista*. In 1229, a Catalan army led by King Jaume I of Aragón and Catalunya took Mallorca. Jaume proved to be an enlightened ruler who profited from the talents of the Moors – those who remained were forcibly converted to Christianity – as well as those of the large Jewish and Genoese trading communities.

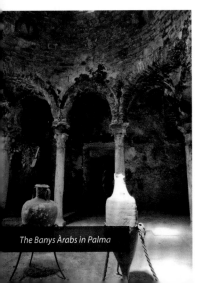

The Banys Àrabs in Palma

Jaume I reigned in Aragón for six decades, but he made the mistake of dividing the lands he had united between his sons. Initially this resulted in the Independent Kingdom of Mallorca, first under Jaume II, then under Sancho and Jaume III. But dynastic rivalry followed, triggering the overthrow of the latter by his cousin, Pedro IV. Attempting to make a comeback, Jaume III was killed in battle near Llucmajor in 1349.

In the following century, the Catholic Monarchs, Ferdinand and Isabella, leading a unified Spain, completed the Reconquest on the Sanish mainland, taking Granada, the only Moorish enclave left on the peninsula, in 1492.

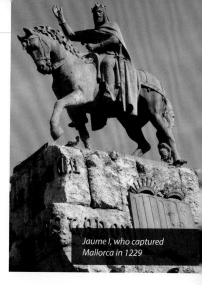
Jaume I, who captured Mallorca in 1229

THE SPANISH EMPIRE

As one tumultuous age ended, another began. Christopher Columbus (Cristobal Colón), the sea-faring captain from Genoa (whom at least three Mallorcan towns claim as their own), believed he could reach the East Indies by sailing westwards. In the same year that Granada fell, Columbus crossed the Atlantic. Spain exported its adventurers, traders and priests, and imposed its language, culture and religion on its colonies, creating a vast empire in the Americas. Ruthless, avaricious conquistadors extracted and sent back incalculable riches in the form of silver and gold. The century and a half following 1492 was known as Spain's Golden Age, but it carried the seeds of its own decline. Plagued by corruption and incompetence, and drained of man-power and ships by such adventurism as the dispatch of the ill-fated *Armada* against England in 1588, Spain was unable to defend her expansive interests.

The Balearic Islands did not benefit much from Spain's glory years. They were forbidden to trade with the Americas, and their existing trade on the eastern routes was interrupted by marauding

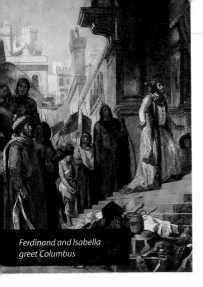

Ferdinand and Isabella greet Columbus

pirates based in North Africa, as well as by the powerful Turkish fleet.

WARS AND CONSEQUENCES

The daughter of Ferdinand and Isabella married the heir to the Holy Roman Emperor, Maximilian of Habsburg. The Spanish crown duly passed to the Habsburgs and remained in their hands until the feeble-minded Carlos II died in 1700, leaving no heir. France seized the chance to install the young grandson of Louis XIV on the Spanish throne. A rival Habsburg claimant was supported by Austria and Britain, who saw a powerful Spanish–French alliance as a major threat. In the subsequent War of the Spanish Succession (1702–13), most of the kingdom of Aragón, including the Balearics, backed the Habsburgs. Britain seized Menorca and retained it, under the Treaty of Utrecht, when the war was over.

By 1805, Spain was once more aligned with France, and Spanish ships fought alongside the French against Admiral Lord Nelson at the Battle of Trafalgar. But Napoleon came to distrust his Spanish ally and forcibly replaced the king of Spain with his own brother, Joseph Bonaparte. A French army marched in to subdue the country. The Spanish resisted and, aided by British troops, commanded by the Duke of Wellington, drove the French out again. What the British call the Peninsular War (1808–14) is known in Spain as the War of Independence.

During the nineteenth century, most of Spain's possessions in the Americas broke away. The Balearics, further neglected, were beset with poverty, and thousands of islanders emigrated to South America in search of a better life. A brief upturn, due to the successful trade in wine, ended when the phylloxera louse destroyed the island's vines.

CRISES, REPUBLIC AND CIVIL WAR

The beginning of the twentieth century in Spain was marked by social and political crises, assassinations and near anarchy. The colonial war in Morocco provided a distraction, but a disastrous defeat there in 1921 led to a coup and the dictatorship of General Primo de Rivera. He fell in 1929, and when elections of 1931 revealed massive anti-royalist feeling, the king followed him into exile.

The new republic was conceived amid an outbreak of strikes and uprisings. In February 1936, the left-wing Popular Front won a majority of seats in the Cortes (parliament), but across Spain,

HOTBED FOR CREATIVITY

Mallorca has always attracted creative people. In 1838, Frédéric Chopin and George Sand spent several months in Valldemossa, during which he composed *The Raindrop Prelude* and she wrote *A Winter in Majorca*. Poet and author Robert Graves came to Deià in 1929 and made it his home; he is buried in the little churchyard on the hill. Agatha Christie stayed at *Hotel Illa d'Or* in Port de Pollença in 1932, which inspired her novel *Problems at Pollensa Bay*. Artist Joan Miró, whose wife Pilar was Mallorcan, set up a house and studio in Palma in 1956, rather than live under the Franco regime and he, too, stayed until his death (in 1983).

localized violence displaced debate. In July 1936, General Francisco Franco staged a coup, which was supported by key military regiments, monarchists, conservatives, the clergy and the right-wing Falangist movement. Aligned on the Republican government's side were liberals, socialists, communists and anarchists. The ensuing Spanish Civil War (1936–39) was brutal and bitter. Support for both sides poured in from outside Spain. Those on the Republican side believed it was a contest between democracy and dictatorship, while Nationalist supporters saw it as a battle between order and communist chaos. During the three years the war lasted, around one million Spaniards lost their lives.

Mallorca and Menorca found themselves on opposite sides. Menorca declared for the Republic, and stayed with it to the bitter end. Mallorca's garrison seized the island for the Nationalists. A decisive factor was the presence in Palma of Italian air squadrons, used to bomb Republican Barcelona.

NEW HORIZONS

Exhausted after the Civil War, Spain remained neutral during World War II and, after the dark years of isolation known as the Noche Negra (Black Night), began a slow economic recovery under Franco's oppressive, law-and-order regime, boosted by the growth of the tourism industry.

A small elite had visited the island in the 1920s, but it was in the late 1950s and early 1960s that northern Europeans first began making sun-seeking pilgrimages to Spain, and the Balearic Islands, in any great numbers. Tourism transformed the impoverished country's economy, landscape and society. Eager to capitalize, government and private interests poured everything into mass tourism, triggering a rash of uncontrolled and indiscriminate building works, with scant regard for tradition or aesthetics. Almost as influential as the financial input was the injection of foreign influences, particularly those associated with the liberalism of the 1960s.

Mallorca, once dependent on agriculture, fishing and small local industries, experienced an explosive growth in tourism and swiftly became one of Europe's most popular holiday destinations.

After the death of General Franco in 1975, his designated successor, the grandson of Alfonso XIII, was crowned King Juan Carlos I. The king managed a smooth transition to democracy, then stood back to allow it full rein. After decades of repression, new freedoms and autonomy were granted to the Spanish regions, and their languages and cultures enjoyed a long-sought renaissance. The Balearic Islands won a degree of autonomy in 1978 and, five years later, became the Comunidad Autónoma de las Islas Baleares. Mallorquín was recognized officially as the language of Mallorca.

*The Spanish and Balearic flags
fly side by side*

MODERNIZATION

Spain joined the European Community (now the European Union) in 1986, which gave a further boost to an expanding economy. Mallorca's tourist industry continued to grow, but so did a realization that lack of planning and good taste was leading to damaging long-term consequences – to the environment and to the island's reputation. By the late 1990s, the 'lager lout' image had become too closely associated with some resorts, production of domestic waste was double the national average, and electricity consumption had increased by 37 percent in five years. It was decided: a new emphasis on quality tourism and safeguarding the environment must take root. Building restrictions were implemented, and a substantial number of areas were declared protected zones.

The economic crisis in 2008 initially saw a downturn in visitor numbers, but since then, things picked up considerably, with Mallorca (along with the other Balearic Islands, Ibiza and Menorca) steadily growing into one of the top tourist destinations in the EU. In 2013, Palma's Pier Ponent was extended to accommodate large cruise ships, and the airport was also enlarged to cope with the burgeoning number of visitors from outside the EU. However, the development was marred by a growing opposition to mass tourism, as well as discontent with the high unemployment rate among the younger population. In 2016, the sustainable tourism tax was implemented, and subsequently increased in 2019, to further protect the island. It's generally reckoned to have been a great success – and is certainly supported by the left-leaning political alliance that has been in power in the Balearics since 2015.

In 2020, Spain and the Balearics were hit hard by Covid-19, and tourism ground to a halt. The following year, the vaccination programme was rolled out, and the epidemic receded. In 2022, all travel restrictions to Spain were discarded, and tourist numbers were back on the rise.

HISTORICAL LANDMARKS

c. 1500BC The islanders learn how to work bronze; the Talayotic period begins.

c. 700BC Carthaginians begin to colonize the Balearics.

123BC–400AD Roman occupation; they name the island Balearis Major and establish towns such as Palmaria (Palma) and Pollentia (Alcúdia).

711 Moors land near Gibraltar, and Spain falls under Islamic rule.

848 Moorish rule imposed in the Balearics; it lasts for 300 years.

1229 Mallorca taken by the Christian army under Jaume I.

1285–87 Alfonso III of Aragón captures Palma.

1349 Jaume III killed in battle by Pere IV of Aragón, ending the Independent Kingdom of Mallorca.

1492 Spain united under the Catholic Monarchs.

1837 First steamship service links Mallorca and Spanish mainland.

1936–39 Spanish Civil War. Mallorca seized by Nationalist forces.

1936–75 Franco's dictatorship; economic hardship in the early years.

1960 Mallorca's airport built. Tourism begins to replace agriculture as the island's main source of income.

1975 Juan Carlos I becomes king after the death of Franco.

1978 Statute of Autonomy gives the Balearic Islands a degree of autonomy; five years later they become an autonomous province and Catalan is restored as the official language.

1986 Spain joins the European Community (now European Union).

1996 The government of the Balearic Islands initiates measures to protect the environment and encourage eco-friendly tourism.

2015 The socialist party (PSIB-PSOE) wins regional elections.

2017 Mallorca passes a law that makes it illegal for bulls to perform for more than ten minutes, or to use sharp implements or have horses in the ring. This makes the sport nearly impossible to stage.

2018 Massive flooding across the eastern part of the island kills at least ten people.

2020 Covid-19 hits Spain hard in the spring.

2021–22 A vaccination programme to protect against Covid-19 is rolled out across Spain, and the epidemic recedes. Tourism picks up again.

Sant Elm, with the island of
Sa Dragonera

OUT AND ABOUT

Although some visitors to this Mediterranean island arrive by ferry from mainland Spain, the majority land at Mallorca international airport, 12km (7.5 miles) outside the capital, Palma de Mallorca. A ring road – the Via Cintura – skirts the city, with roads branching off to the rest of the island; to the craggy, beautiful northwest coast, the quiet, friendly towns peppering the interior plain, the wetlands of S'Albufera in the north, the tiny calas in the east, and the tourist-dominated strips to the east and west of Palma.

Tour agencies offer excursions, by coach or boat, or a combination of the two, to hidden beaches, mountain villages, spectacular caves and weekly markets, but hiring a car (see page 117) is the best way to get around the island. The railway options are currently rather limited – the T1 runs to Inca, while the T2 continues to Sa Pobla in the north and the T3 heads to Manacor in the east. There is also the tourist railway that trundles along the picturesque route from Palma to Sóller. Bus services throughout Mallorca are comprehensive and reliable (see page 131).

PALMA DE MALLORCA

Hooking around a sheltered bay, **Palma ❶** is a large, cosmopolitan city, with around 405,000 inhabitants – nearly half the permanent population of Mallorca. It is very much a Mediterranean city, with gently nodding palm trees and bushes of fragrant oleander, outdoor cafés with colourful awnings, and gleaming yachts and working vessels bobbing alongside one another in the bay. Palma is a capital with a long history, as the Gothic cathedral towering above the city walls indicates as you approach from the airport. It's smart and urbane, with a clutch of designer boutiques, chic restaurants and contemporary art galleries. Come sundown, it's a lively city that stays awake long into the night too.

The old quarter wrapping around the cathedral is perched on a small hill overlooking the bay, and its narrow, atmospheric streets are full of unexpected surprises, from tiny, traditional shops to hidden taverns and hole-in-the-wall bars. To the east of the centre is the Platja de Palma, a long necklace of sandy beaches that's sadly been scarred by a stretch of concrete from Ca'n Pastilla to S'Arenal. To the west is the seaside promenade of modern Palma, where luxury hotels peer out over a clanking copse of yacht masts, although separated from the harbour by a stretch of six-lane highway. Crowning the wooded slopes above the city, where the Spanish royal family have a summer home, are the stone towers of the Castell de Bellver (see page 40).

Palma's cathedral keeps watch over the harbour

THE CATHEDRAL

Standing proud above the city walls, spectacular when illuminated at night, is the **Catedral Ⓐ** (www. catedraldemallorca.org; April–May Mon–Fri 10am–5.15pm, June–Sept Mon–Fri 10am–6.15pm, Nov–March Mon–Fri 10am–3.15pm, Sat year round 10am–2.15pm; entered via the museum). Also known as **La Seu**, it is one of the finest Gothic churches in Spain. Construction began in 1230

La Seu, or Catedral

by Jaume I, on the site of the Great Mosque after the Christians recaptured the island from the Moors, but it took nearly four centuries to complete. Densely packed flying buttresses on the south facade create an extraordinary effect, especially in the glow of the setting sun, when they are reflected in the lake of Parc de la Mar.

The fourteenth-century **Portal del Mirador**, on the same building flank, is a feast of carved stone figurines, including a depiction of *The Last Supper*. Entry via the Portal de l'Almoina, below the square. Before you go in, pause to admire the splendid view of the Bay of Palma from the **Mirador** to the south.

The **Museu del Catedral** (hours as above) contains a splendid silver monstrance, some interesting medieval paintings and a handful of holy relics. An early Renaissance doorway in carved stone leads into the Baroque Chapter House. The vault of the cathedral's three-aisled, 121m (396ft) interior is supported by slim, elegant pillars. The largest of the seven **rose windows** is magnificent,

Guided tours

In summer, a number of guided tours cover aspects such as *Modernisme*, the Jewish Quarter, the patios, a night tour, and one called Palma Monumental that gives a good historical background. Pick up leaflets from one of the tourist offices.

12m (40ft) across, composed of 1,236 separate sections of stained glass. The extraordinary *baldachin*, a wrought-iron crown of thorns over the high altar, was added by Catalan *Moderniste* architect Antoni Gaudí, creator of Barcelona's Sagrada Família, who worked for ten years on the cathedral in the early twentieth century, though his visits were often short-lived. (*Modernisme* is the Catalan version of Art Nouveau.) The tombs of Jaume II and Jaume III, fourteenth-century kings of Catalunya and Mallorca, are in the Capella de la Trinitat at the east end. The Capella del Santissim is covered with innovative ceramics by Mallorcan artist Miquel Barceló – the result of six years' work before its much-awaited unveiling in February 2007.

To the east of the Catedral is the **Museu Diocesà** (the same hours as the cathedral), back in its permanent home in the Bishop's Palace. It contains medieval and Gothic statuary and paintings, along with some lovely stained-glass windows by Gaudí, who lived in the palace while he worked on the Catedral. The palace itself is well worth a look, too.

PALAU DE L'ALMUDAINA

The **Palau de l'Almudaina** Ⓑ (Tues–Sun April–Sept 10am–8pm, Oct–March until 6pm; free to EU citizens summer Wed–Thurs 5–8pm, winter 3–5pm; www.patrimonionacional.es) stands just opposite of the cathedral. Once the residence of the Moorish emirs, then of the medieval kings of Mallorca, it is an aesthetic blend of Islamic and Catalan-Gothic architecture. Highlights include the stone-vaulted throne room, a pretty courtyard (Patio del Rei), a Gothic chapel (Capella de Santa Anna), and heavily restored royal offices, sometimes used by the present king, where traces of early paintwork survive on the ceilings and walls. There is also a clutch of impressive fifteenth- and sixteenth-century Flemish tapestries.

AROUND THE HISTORIC CENTRE

In Carrer Palau Reial, to the north of the Almudaina, where brightly painted horse-drawn carriages wait for customers (when a heat alert is in place, they are forbidden from working between noon and 5pm), is another palace, which houses the **Palau March Museu** Ⓒ (www.fundacionbmarch.es; Mon–Fri April–Oct

Palau de l'Almudaina

10am–6.30pm, Nov–March 10am–5pm, Sat 10am–2pm). Within this majestic building and its courtyard is a small but superb collection of contemporary sculpture, including works by Henry Moore, Barbara Hepworth, Rodin and Chillida, and murals by the Catalan artist Josep Maria Sert. Check the website for details of any upcoming temporary exhibitions. The palace is also a venue for classical concerts in spring and summer.

The ochre colonnades of the Parliament Building – **Parlament de les Illes Baleares** – run along nearly the full length of Carrer Palau Reial. At the far end, the opulent Renaissance facade of the **Ajuntament** (Town Hall), its overhanging wooden eaves supported by carved beams, dominates **Plaça Cort**. You can go inside to see the huge processional figures that are stored here. In the centre of the square is an ancient, gnarled olive tree, a favourite spot for photos.

Basílica de Sant Francesc

Turn right from the *plaça* and you will reach a pleasant little square, named for the fourteenth-century church of **Santa Eulàlia Ⓓ**, which has a Gothic nave, altar paintings by Francisco Gomez and a clutch of Baroque chapels. Behind the church in the narrow Carrer Can Sanç (off Carrer Carnisseria) is **Can Joan de S'Aigo** (www.canjoandesaigo.com; daily 8am–9pm), a beautifully tiled café, which was artist Joan Miró's favourite place for hot chocolate and almond cake, and popular with everyone for ice cream.

A right turn brings you to Plaça Quadrado, shaded by palms and plane trees, and with a string of attractive *Moderniste* buildings, the best one being Can Barceló (1902). Above the third-floor oriel windows, the facade is decorated with mosaics portraying domestic scenes with women and children. The massive thirteenth-century **Basílica de Sant Francesc** 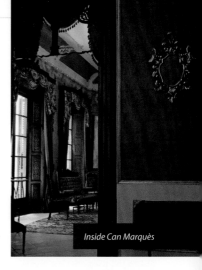 (Mon–Sat 9.30am–12.30pm & 3.10pm–6pm, Sun & bank holidays 9am–noon) backs onto Quadrado, and looms above the adjoining Plaça Sant Francesc. A sculpture outside depicts Mallorcan missionary Fray Juníper Serra, founder of the first Californian missions (see page 70). Inside the church, to the left of the Baroque altar, a side-chapel contains the alabaster tomb of Catalan scholar, mystic and missionary Ramón Llull (1235–1316). But the main event is the enchanting Gothic cloister (through which you enter the church), with slender columns, delicate tracery, and lemon trees around a central fountain.

Inside Can Marquès

PATIOS AND MUSEUMS

The old quarter of Palma is rich in Renaissance mansions, most dating from the sixteenth to the eighteenth centuries, with wonderful patios concealed behind their great wooden doors. With ornate staircases, decorated tiles, palms and potted plants, sometimes cooled by small fountains, they are a delight. Among the best are Can Olesa on Carrer Morey, Can Tacón on Carrer de Sant Jaume II, and Can Bordils (Palma Municipal Archive) and Can Oms, both on Carrer Almudaina.

Most are private or commercial properties, and you have to be content with peeping through the gateways. Alternatively, you can explore a couple of these patios by visiting the museums housed within. On Carrer de la Portella, the renovated Renaissance **Ca La Gran Cristiana** houses the **Museu de Mallorca** (www.museude-mallorca.caib.es; Mon–Fri 10am–6pm, Sat & Sun 11am–2pm). Exhibits include thirteenth- to sixteenth-century religious paintings, *Moderniste* tiles and twentieth-century paintings. The prehistory and classical archaeology rooms were undergoing a long-term refurbishment at the time of writing.

The former private mansion Can Marqués on Carrer Apuntadors is now the newly renovated five-star hotel **Palacio Can Marquès**. Originally fifteenth century, the house was mostly furnished and decorated in bourgeois, nineteenth-century style, with some interesting *Moderniste* additions. Following careful renovation, it has been converted into thirteen unique and luxurious suites, with the interiors designed by New York-based Aline Matsika.

Not far away, on Carrer Can Serra, are the **Banys Àrabs** ⑤ (Arab Baths; daily 10am–5.30pm), still standing after 1000 years. The courtyard garden is a tranquil, beautiful place when it's not filled with excursion groups. Late afternoon is a good time to visit.

MODERNISTE SITES

Alternatively, retrace your steps to Plaça Cort, from where it is only a short walk to the intriguing little shopping streets of Carrer Colom and Jaume II, both of which lead to the deep yellow facades and green shutters of the former market place, the **Plaça Major** ⑤.

The square is busy with cafés, street entertainers and handicraft stalls selling scarves, jewellery and batik work.

Approaching the square, you pass the **Plaça Marquès del Palmer**, where there are two excellent examples of *Moderniste* architecture – Can Rei and L'Àguila, adorned with ornate iron grill-work and colourful ceramic flourishes; a café and a smart shoe shop occupy the ground floors.

Down a flight of steps from the Plaça Major, lined with tourist-trap kiosks, is Plaça Weyler, with another pair of fine examples of *Modernisme*. The major one is the imposing **Gran Hotel ⑪**, now reimagined as a cultural centre by the **Fundació La Caixa** (www.fundacionlacaixa.org; Tues–Sat 10am–8pm, Sun 11am–2pm). It includes a bookshop, a smart café-restaurant and an art centre that stages excellent exhibitions of contemporary works – home-grown and international – and has a permanent display of the work of Catalan painter Hermen Anglada Camarasa (1872–1959), who lived in Pollença. This was one of the first modern hotels in Mallorca, built in 1903 by Lluís Doménech i Muntaner. Following a chequered history, La Caixa (Spain's third-largest financial institution) bought it in 1987 and, after hefty renovation works, it reopened in 1993.

Across from the *Gran Hotel* is a small bakery and

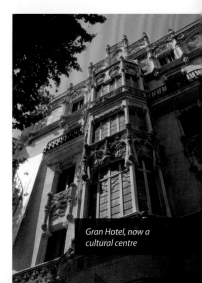

Gran Hotel, now a cultural centre

The Forn des Teatre

café, the **Forn des Teatre** (www.fornetdelasoca.com), whose graceful facade graces many a postcard. Down the street, on Plaça Mercat, stand the two gently undulating *Moderniste* buildings that comprise **Can Casasayas**. The bakery took its name from the neighbouring **Teatre Principal**, a grand edifice that stages excellent plays, operas and concerts (see page 92). Follow the road past the theatre and you reach **Via Roma**, an avenue called La Rambla after Barcelona's promenade.

CARRER SANT MIQUEL

Turn right from Plaça Major, instead of descending the steps, and you will be swallowed up by the bustle of Carrer Sant Miquel, a busy pedestrianized shopping street. Here, too, the **Museu Fundació Joan March ❶** (www.march.es; Mon–Fri 10am–6.30pm, Sat 10.30am–2pm; guided tours available; free) is located. This striking eighteenth-century building, with marble staircases and stained glass, houses an exceptional collection belonging to the wealthy March banking family. The seventy-strong permanent collection includes works by Picasso, Miró, Dalí, Tàpies and Juan Gris.

Heading north up the street, you will come to the church of **Sant Miquel** (Mon–Sat 8am–13.30pm & 5pm–7.30pm, Sun 10am–12.30pm & 6pm–7.30pm). This ancient church is the religious heart of the neighbourhood, a solid building with a fine Baroque altarpiece. A little further on is the deconsecrated church of **Sant Antoniet**, whose pretty courtyard plays host to a variety of temporary art exhibitions (Mon–Fri 10am–2pm & 3.30pm–8pm, Sat 10am–1.30pm), and the walls and pavement outside have become an informal gallery space for local emerging street artists.

Round the corner, on the right, is the **Mercat de l'Olivar ❼** (www.mercatolivar.com; Mon–Thurs 7am–2.30pm, Fri 7am–8pm, Sat 7am–3pm), the city's largest fish, meat and produce market. A very short distance further along Carrer Caputxins is the Plaça d'Espanya, where you will find the Estació Intermodal, the combined rail and bus station.

PASSEIG D'ES BORN TO THE WATERFRONT

If you swerve west instead of north from Plaça Weyler, along traffic-filled Carrer Unió, you come to Plaça Rei Joan Carles I. Ahead is the busy shopping street, Avinguda Jaume III; to your left, the

CULTURAL LEGACY

The Fundació March was set up by the extremely wealthy March banking dynasty in 1955 as a philanthropic institution to promote science and culture. You will see branches of the Banca March all over the Balearic Islands, and notice their name appended to numerous cultural ventures. As well as the two major museums mentioned here, there is an extensive library and archive in the Palau March, open to the public as well, and concerts are held there in summer. The foundation also funds an annual programme of twentieth-century classical music at Palma's Auditorio and summer concerts in the Jardins March in Cala Ratjada, where there is some splendid modern sculpture. Annual prizes for literary criticism and short novels are also awarded by the bank.

Shopping at the market

leafy **Passeig des Born**. This broad central avenue, lined with benches and guarded at either end by a pair of stone sphinxes, runs down to **Plaça de la Reina** , dominated by a large central fountain. At No. 27, the elegant eighteenth-century **Palau Solleric** (www.casalsolleric.palma.cat; Tues–Sat 11am–2pm & 3.30pm–8.30pm, Sun 11am–2.30pm; free) houses a cultural foundation and hosts contemporary art exhibitions, plus it also has a café and a tourist information desk.

To the left of Plaça de la Reina (past the tourist office), steps lead back up to the cathedral. Hugging the old city walls is **S'Hort del Rei**, a lovely Arabic-style garden, dotted with fountains and pools, which makes a pleasant distraction from city traffic. Miró's beloved **Personatge** sculpture, *The Egg*, stands on the corner nearest the *plaça*. Facing it is the cool and minimalist café that is part of the Palau March. Parallel to S'Hort del Rei, a much-needed carpark was built beneath a stretch of the Avinguda Antoni Maura.

Beneath the city walls, on the southern side, the attractively landscaped **Parc de la Mar** forms a barrier against the coastal motorway, the **Passeig Marítim**. The park has an artificial lake and is dotted with modern sculptures, including works by Miró. It is the venue for free open-air concerts on summer evenings, as is Ses Voltes, lying directly beneath the Catedral walls.

A right turn here leads to the turreted **Sa Llotja** Ⓛ (www.palma. cat; open only if there are exhibitions; free) in the square of the same name. Designed in the fifteenth century by Guillem Sagrera (after whom this stretch of the Passeig Marítim is named), it was once the merchants' stock exchange, and is one of Spain's finest civic Gothic buildings, with slim columns twisting through a light-flooded interior to the vaulted roof. It is now used for art exhibitions. Nearby, **Plaça Drassana** is a pleasant if somewhat shabby neighbourhood square. Back on the main coastal road, the seventeenth-century **Consolat de Mar**, the former maritime law court, is the HQ of the president of the Balearic Islands' government. The two buildings are linked by the Porta del Mar, one of the old city gates. The maze of narrow streets between Plaça de Sa Llotja and Plaça de la Reina forms Palma's lively restaurant and nightlife area.

Cross the road at the nearest traffic lights to explore Palma's harbour and waterfront. You will probably spot some fishermen mending their nets (although the fishing fleet is not what it was), smart yachts around the **Real Club Náutic** (www.rcnp.es), opportunities to take trips around the harbour, and, at the western end, the car ferry passenger terminal. En route, several pleasant cafés and restaurants gaze out over the port, while cyclists, runners and rollerbladers

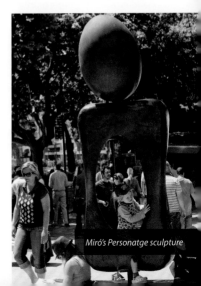

Miró's Personatge sculpture

whizz past on a designated track. The harbourfront is planted with palms, hibiscus and oleander, but there is no ignoring the fact that six lanes of traffic are roaring past on the other side. Despite this, it is very pleasant on a summer evening, when the sun sets over the water and the illuminated cathedral glows before you.

Back from the waterfront, almost opposite the Real Club Náutic, is the prestigious **Es Baluard Museu d'Art Modern i Contemporani** Ⓜ (www.esbaluard.org; Tues–Sat 10am–8pm, Sun 10am–3pm), housed in a stunning white structure built into the city fortifications in Plaça Porta de Santa Catalina. Its temporary exhibitions change regularly and are a fascinating reason to visit, but it also has permanent works by Picasso, Miró and Tàpies as well as Mallorcan artists Miquel Barceló and Juli Ramis on display. The views of the port and the city from the museum's rooftop and terrace are impressive. Classical music recitals are held in the museum on some evenings.

OUT-OF-TOWN ATTRACTIONS

Further west, there are three more places worth mentioning. The **Poble Espanyol** Ⓝ (www.puebloespanolmallorca.com; Nov–March 9am–5pm, April–Oct 10am–6pm), a walled town of replica architectural treasures from across Spain, is kitsch but entertaining. The buildings house shops, craft studios, bars and cafés. It is reached on foot (20 minutes from the city centre) or by bus Nos 5, 29, 46 (Andrea Doria bus stop) and 50 (Bus Turistic).

Just south of the Poble Espanyol, perched on a hilltop, is the **Castell de Bellver** Ⓞ (www.castelldebellver.palma.cat; April–Sept Tues–Sat until 7pm, Sun 10am–3pm, Oct–March Tues–Sat 10am–6pm, Sun 10am–3pm; free on Sundays; guided tours in English Tues–Sat at 11am; a minimum of five persons is required), reached on bus No 50 (Bus Turistic). A magnificent example of Gothic military architecture, the castle has commanded the approaches to the city since the fourteenth century. From the battlements, the view of the city and the bay is quite stunning. Inside, the small **Museu d'Història de la Ciutat** traces the history and archaeology of the area.

The best of the three is the **Fundació Pilar i Joan Miró** Ⓟ (www.miromallorca.com; Tues–Sat mid-May to mid-Sept 10am–7pm, mid-Sept to mid-May 10am–6pm, Sun 10am–3pm all year; free on Saturdays 3pm–6pm & first Sun of each month) on Carrer Joan de Saridakis in the suburb of Cala Major. Bus No 4 or 46 will take you right to the door, but a taxi from the centre is not too expensive. The Catalan artist and his Mallorcan wife lived on the island, from 1956 until his death in 1983, and the foundation displays a fine selection of his work.

WESTERN CORNER OF MALLORCA

When tourism hit Mallorca, the Bay of Palma, with two magnificent sweeps of white sand almost 30km (18 miles) long, was irresistible, and the resorts that mushroomed along here in the 1960s and 1970s gave the island a name for cheap and cheerful holidays. The picture soon turned decidedly tacky, dominated by package tourism and high-rise hotels, though in recent years, the Balearic

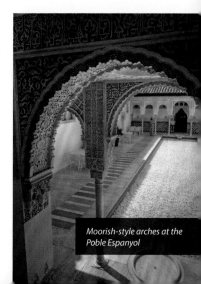

Moorish-style arches at the Poble Espanyol

Portals Vells

government has done its best to move everything more upmarket.

To the west of the bay, there's less intense development after Camp de Mar, where the coast road winds through forest to Port d'Andratx. After a detour to Sant Elm, at the island's southwestern tip, there is a beautiful winding coast road to the village of Banyalbufar. Then, you can head inland via the La Granja estate and La Reserva Puig de Galatzó, after which you can complete the loop back to Palma, or continue up the picturesque west coast.

WEST OF THE BAY

You can either take the Via Cintura (ring road Ma-20), which becomes the Ma-1 motorway at Porto Pi, or the coast road. Either way, you will see a turn-off to Cala Major (where the Spanish royal family have their summer home). The coast road wends through the resorts of Sant Agustí, with its small yacht harbour, and crowded Ses Illetes, to a rocky stretch of coast and the exclusive Bendinat and Portals Nous. Here, apartments cluster on the slopes and a glamorous marina, Puerto Portals, has been carved out of the cliffs.

Sandy beaches start again at the resorts of Costa d'en Blanes – where the popular aquarium, Marineland, is situated – and Palma Nova. The latter blends almost imperceptibly into big, brash

Magaluf. The wide, sandy beach here abounds with a solid block of bronzing bodies by day; the town centre is an equally solid stretch of drinkers by night. This is tourism overkill: vast bars and discos, waterparks, restaurants offering frankfurters, curry and all-day English breakfasts, widescreen televized football and some of the coarsest shops imaginable. Recent years have seen significant pushback on some of the area's unchecked tourism and overly rowdy partygoers.

A pine-flanked road runs south to the pretty cove of **Portals Vells ❷**, which has somehow escaped overdevelopment. The cliffs are honeycombed with huge caverns dating from prehistoric times, enlarged over the centuries. Boats make the short excursion from the pier at Magaluf, so it's not always peaceful. Its neighbour, El Mago, was Mallorca's first nudist beach. Not far south of Portals Vells, you can walk to the tranquil cove of **Cala Figuera** (one of three coves on the island with this name), but the end of the peninsula is an abandoned military base almost entirely cloaked in graffiti. Discussions are ongoing about whether to demolish it.

PORT D'ANDRATX AND SANT ELM

Back at Magaluf, pick up the motorway and turn off at Camp de Mar, where a scenic road twists through pine forest to **Port d'Andratx ❸**. More yachts than fishing boats bob on the calm waters of the bay these days. The old harbour area still looks traditional, but a string of chic restaurants and

Labyrinth of lanes

Even disreputable Magaluf has been going upmarket. Exclusive private beach club Nikki Beach (tel: 971 123 962; www.mallorca.nikkibeach.com) has opened here along with some luxury hotels from Meliá, including the *Sol Wave House* (tel: 971 131 624; www.melia.com), which has surf machines and DJs on the terrace.

Port d'Andratx

shops lines the waterfront, and villas and apartments climb the slopes across the water. The lack of a sandy beach has kept the big hotels and package tours away, however, and Port d'Andratx feels relaxed.

The quiet inland town of Andratx plays host to the impressive **CCA Andratx Art Contemporani** (www.ccandratx.com; March–Oct Tues–Fri 10.30am–7pm, Sat & Sun 10.30am–4pm, Nov–Feb Tues–Sun 10.30am–4pm), the brainchild of a cool Danish couple, which stages art exhibitions and runs artists' workshops. This is the largest contemporary art centre in Mallorca, and well worth a stop on any cultural itinerary.

From here, you could make a detour to **Sant Elm ④**, the island's westernmost point, a former fishing village that has clung on to its identity, though sailors, surfers and divers have known about it for a long time. Offshore, the nature-reserve island of **Sa Dragonera** (www.balearsnarura.com) can be visited almost every day by boat. Check the boat company's website for departure details (www.crucerosmargarita.com).

UP THE SCENIC COAST

From Andratx, the Ma-10 runs across the southern reaches of the **Serra de Tramuntana**, around numerous hairpin bends to the coast, where it weaves between the ocean and the clifftops. To the right are terraces planted with fruit trees and olives, and a string of delightful little villages. Along the road are a succession of *miradors*, lookout points with commanding views of the entire coast; one or two still crowned with ancient watchtowers from which lookouts once scanned the sea for pirate ships. The **Mirador Es Grau ❺** has fantastic views of the coast, and a huge restaurant in which to sit and enjoy them.

Estellencs, some 4km (2.5 miles) on, is an ancient village, set amid orange groves on the slopes of Puig de Galatzó (1,027m/3,370ft). From the town, you can walk or drive down a track to a little fishing cove. Another 5km (3 miles) further on, one of the finest views of the coast can be had from the sixteenth-century tower of the **Torre del Verger**. The next town, **Banyalbufar ❻**, is a pretty place with Moorish origins. The Arabic name means 'vineyard by the sea', and it is still famous for its terraced hillsides – and a popular haunt for artists. There are a couple of pleasant hotels, a cluster of restaurants, and a lane that twists down to a rocky cove whose crystal-clear water is ideal for diving.

LA GRANJA

North of Banyalbufar, the road turns inland, in the direction of **Esporles**, close to which you'll find the estate of **La Granja ❼** (www.lagranja.net; daily 10am–7pm, winter until 6pm). It is a bit of a theme park, but still worth a visit. In Roman times, the estate was renowned for the purity of its water, and there is still

The manor house at La Granja

a scattering of fountains in the leafy gardens. The interior of the house is magnificent and gives a good idea of how the landed classes once lived. The chapel and the torture chamber speak for themselves. The donkeys, pigs, wild goats and sheep in the grounds are usually a hit with children; you might even witness a black vulture soaring overhead, too. There are tastings of fig bread and local cheese and sausages. From February until October, there is a craft and horse show on Wednesday and Friday at 4pm, while Thursdays have performances of regional music, folk dancing and dressage at 4pm.

From here, you can return to Palma on the Ma-1120, continue up the west coast, or take the minor road to Puigpunyent to visit **La Reserva Puig de Galatzó** ❽ (daily 10am–6pm; last admittance two hours before closing). A tangle of 3km (2 miles) of paths wraps around waterfalls and caves, weaving through protected land rich in bird and animal life, on the lush slopes of Galatzó, known as the mystical mountain because of its magnetic properties. The paths are fairly easy, though you will need sensible shoes. If you want something more adventurous, you can try abseiling, climbing, mountain biking, zip-lining and crossing rope bridges – although these so-called 'Adventure Trails' are quite expensive.

THE WEST COAST

This is one of the most dramatic and beautiful routes in Mallorca. It's hard to pick a highlight as there are so many, from Valldemossa, where George Sand and Frédéric Chopin once stayed, to the lovely hilltop village of Deià, the former home of poet Robert Graves, the clifftop mansion of the Habsburg Archduke Ludwig, and the agreeable town of Sóller.

Whether you are continuing a route round the coast on the Ma-10 or coming direct from Palma on the Ma-1110 – a good, relatively straight road, running through groves of olives and almonds – your first stop will be Valldemossa. As you approach, the incline becomes steeper until the village and monastery suddenly appear, like something out of a fairy tale.

LA REAL CARTUJA DE VALLDEMOSSA

Although **Valldemossa** ❾ was the birthplace of Mallorca's only home-grown saint, Catalina Tomás, it was the visit of French writer George Sand – Amandine-Aurore-Lucile Dupin – and her lover, Frédéric Chopin, in the winter of 1838–39 that really put the town on the map. They don't seem to have been very happy here, however; Chopin was unwell, the weather was miserable, and the villagers disapproved of Sand's habit of wearing men's clothes and smoking cigars. She disparaged the local people in her book, *A Winter in Majorca*, calling them 'barbarians and thieves', although she thought Mallorca 'the most beautiful place I have ever lived'.

Valldemossa monastery

Nowadays, coachloads of visitors disturb the peace of this little hilltop town as they flock to see the couple's lodgings in the former Carthusian monastery, **La Real Cartuja de Valldemossa** (www.cartoixadevalldemossa.com; April–Sept Mon–Sat 9.30am–7pm, Sun 10am–1pm, Oct Mon–Sat 9.30am–6pm, Sun 10am–1pm, Nov & Feb Mon–Sat 9.30am–5.30pm, early Dec & mid- to late Jan Mon–Sat 9.30am–3.30pm, but check opening hours on website before your visit as they can fluctuate). The monastery was founded in 1399, but when the monks were expelled in 1835, some of their cells were sold as apartments – the 'cells' were, in fact, three-room suites with private gardens. Those rented by Sand and Chopin are now a museum, which displays manuscripts, Chopin's death mask and his piano. You can also visit the massive church, the pharmacy with a beautiful collection of eighteenth-century ceramic jars, the library and the Prior's Cell. There is an interesting **Museu Municipal** here, too, with documents relating to the Archduke Ludwig; and an **art gallery** displaying paintings by Joan Miró, Max Ernst and Antoni Saura as well as Mallorcan landscapes.

The adjoining sixteenth-century palace, the **Palau Sancho** (hours as for La Cartuja, closes half an hour later; combined ticket), was constructed on the site of one that Jaume II built for his son, Sancho, and is entered via a tranquil, plant-filled courtyard. Piano recitals of Chopin's music are held throughout the day, and Festival Chopin takes place here every August.

AROUND THE TOWN

Outside the monastery is a cobbled *plaça* shaded with lime trees – *tilos* – which give the square its name. The streets around it, and those leading to the thirteenth-century church of Sant Bartomeu, dedicated to Santa Catalina, are bright with potted plants, and the steepest, most slippery parts are covered with strips of carpet to prevent people tripping up.

The main street in the lower town, where there are adequate carparks, is lined with cafés and restaurants and some interesting little shops, selling jewellery and clothes made of cool, natural fibres. One of the nicest bars, set just back from the main street, on Carrer Blanquera, serves delicious *horchata* (rice-based drink), fresh juice, good coffee and hot chocolate, along with *cocas de patata*, the sugar-dusted, potato-shaped buns, tasting not unlike *ensaïmadas*, that are a local speciality.

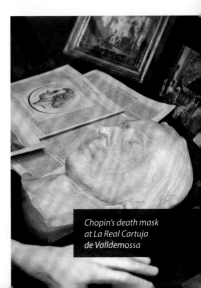

Chopin's death mask at La Real Cartuja de Valldemossa

In the other direction, a few metres along the road towards Banyalbufar, a vertiginous road plummets 6km (4 miles) to the tiny **Port de Valldemossa** where there's a small gravel beach and crystal-clear water. On summer weekends, however, the narrow road and the limited parking area become uncomfortably busy.

SON MARROIG

The coastal Ma-10 nudges north, with stunning sea views to the left, and groves of ancient, gnarled olive trees among huge boulders to the right. After about 6km (4 miles), a track signposted simply **Miramar** leads to the ruins of a monastery founded by Ramon Lull. Only part of the cloister remains, but there is also a chapel and a museum with artefacts collected by Archduke Ludwig. A short way further on, a sign points to **Son Marroig ⑩** (www.sonmarroig. com; Mon–Sat April–Sept 9.30am–7pm, Oct–March 10am–6pm), a manor house that belonged to the Austrian Archduke Ludwig Salvator of Habsburg-Lorraine and Bourbon, who had a life-long love affair with the Balearics and their people. Born in Florence in 1847, he renounced courtly life in Vienna and spent years travelling the world on scientific explorations, returning often to the estate

CATALINA TOMÁS

Santa Catalina is Mallorca's very own saint. She was born in Valldemossa in 1531 in a house at Carrer Rectoría 5, behind the church, and this is now a tiny shrine. In a quiet corner of Carrer de la Beatà, where caged birds sing, there is another smaller shrine with a fountain and ferns. Almost every house has a tiled picture outside, depicting scenes from the saint's life and asking her blessing: 'Santa Catalina Tomás Pregau Per Nosaltres'. She was a farmer's daughter, marked out as special when still a child, and taken to Palma by a sympathetic patron, where she worked as a servant in a wealthy household before entering the convent of Santa Magdalena and taking her vows.

Deià clings to the slopes of the Teix massif

he bought in 1870 on this beautiful stretch of coast. Several rooms, filled with paintings, photos and ceramics, can be visited. In the gardens, there's a wonderful view from a cliffedge white temple made of Carrara marble.

Hundreds of metres below the house is **Sa Foradada**, a rocky promontory, pierced by a remarkable 18m (60ft)-wide natural window. If you visit the house, ask for permission to make the half-hour walk down to the sea and the landing stage where the Archduke used to anchor his yacht, the *Nixe*. The restaurant near the carpark is a wonderful place from which to watch the sunset. For details of concerts at Son Marroig during the Deià International Music Festival, see page 95.

DEIÀ

Clinging to the slopes of the 1,064m (3,491ft) Teix massif, **Deià** ⓫ is a delight, a pretty town of honey-coloured stone that has lured artists, writers and assorted expatriates ever since the Archduke Ludwig first came here. He was followed by the Catalan poet and painter Santiago Rusinyol at the turn of the twentieth century, and later by writer Anaïs Nin (1903–77) and American archaeologist William Waldren. But it is Robert Graves (1895–1985), the poet and author of *I, Claudius* and the autobiographical *Goodbye to All That*, who visited with American writer Laura Riding in 1929, that is most closely associated with the place. Graves loved Deià and fiercely defended the northwest coast against commercial exploitation. His home, **Ca N'Alluny** (tel: 971 636 185; www.lacasaderobertgraves.org; April–Oct Mon–Fri 10am–5pm, Sat 10am–3pm, Nov & Feb–March Mon–Fri 9am–4pm, Sat until 2pm, Dec & Jan Mon–Fri 10.30am–1.30pm) on the Carretera Deià–Sóller, has been restored and opened as a museum. The house and garden are delightful, and retain much of their original character as well as exhibiting the writer's effects.

You must leave your car on the main street, which is lined with restaurants, galleries and shops. Narrow, winding streets lead to the top of the village and the little church of **Sant Joan Baptista**. Beside it is a small cemetery overlooking the Mediterranean; a simple cement slab bears the inscription 'Robert Graves, Poeta, E.P.D.'.

Deià is extremely popular, and a well-heeled crowd have set up holiday homes here. Besides a luxury hotel, *Belmond La Residencia* (www.belmond.com), there is a handful of wallet-friendly alternatives (see page 136), and the best selection of restaurants on the coast (see page 109).

CALA DEIÀ

Just past the village, a twisting 2km (1 mile) drive takes you down to **Cala Deià**, a tiny cove with a rocky beach, where ramps emerge from boathouses set into the cliffs. The water is clear and safe, and there are a couple of reasonable beach cafés. Don't imagine you've

Cala de Deià

found a secluded beach, though. Regular visitors know it well, and it can get very busy at weekends. You can walk to the beach, either by following steps near the vehicle-access road, or by walking down steep Carrer Bauza at the Valldemossa end of the village, tracing the course of a stream past pretty gardens until the village peters out, and the path continues through groves of lemons and olives; it takes about thirty-five minutes in all.

SÓLLER AND ITS PORT

From Deià, the coast road, lined with groves of oranges, lemons and almonds as well as olives, descends into the broad valley of Sóller. The scenery is lovely, and the town of **Sóller** ⑫ itself is a little gem, a busy, prosperous place that claims, like several others, to have been the birthplace of Columbus. It is full of well-preserved eighteenth- and nineteenth-century mansions, and the main, café-lined square, **Plaça Sa Constitució**, is a good place to sit and

Sóller's vintage tram

absorb the town's character. Like the old main street, the Gran Via, the square has *Moderniste* (Catalan Art Nouveau) flourishes, including the church of **Sant Bartomeu**, and the former Banco Central Hispano (now Banco Santander) on the opposite corner, whose exteriors were designed by a pupil of Antoni Gaudí. About five minutes' walk to the east is **Can Prunera** (Carrer de sa Lluna 86; www.canprunera.com; daily 10.30am–6.30pm, Nov–Feb Tues–Sun 10.30am–6pm), a fine old mansion which has been converted into a museum dedicated to the *Moderniste* movement.

The train station at the top of the town is another splendid *Moderniste* building. You can make an old-fashioned journey on a little wooden train that has been running to Palma on a narrow-gauge railway since 1912 (Tren de Sóller; journey time about an hour; www.trendesoller.com).

The station has another attraction, too: the **Sala Miró y Sala Picasso** (daily 10.30am–6.30pm; free), hung with drawings and lithographs by Miró and filled with a display of some fifty ceramic pieces by Picasso.

Outside the station, you can get information on hiking *(senderisme)* from the tourist office (tel: 971 638 458 or 971 638 008), housed in an old train carriage. Here, too, you can catch the vintage **tram** that rattles on a scenic, twenty-minute journey to **Port de**

Sóller (www.trendesoller.com; departs every hour 8am–8.30pm; tickets sold on board), stopping en route where requested. The port is a good old-fashioned resort, with a fine harbour, and it has gained a crop of smart restaurants and bars in recent years. You can hire kayaks, sign up for sailing or windsurfing lessons, and take scenic boat trips around the bay or further afield to Sa Calobra and Sa Foradada.

TWO GARDENS

Just outside town, beside the ring road, is the **Museu Balear de Ciències Naturals i Jardí Botànic** (www.museucienciesnaturals. org; March–Oct Tues–Sat 10am–6pm, Nov–Feb Tues–Sat 10am–2pm), planted with a collection of aromatic herbs and plants from all over the Balearic Islands, fossils, a vegetable garden and a 'peace garden'.

The road from Sóller to Palma, with numerous hairpin bends negotiating the 496m (1,627ft) **Coll de Sóller**, was believed to be impeding the local economy and consequently, in the 1990s, a tunnel was drilled through the mountains. This slashed travel time to Palma to around half an hour; a private company built the tunnel and made a fortune from a tunnel toll, though the toll fee was removed in 2017.

At the southern exit from the tunnel (on the left) are the **Jardins d'Alfàbia** ⓭

Tipico de Sóller

Sóller is a good place to try freshly squeezed orange juice (zumo de naranja), as the orange groves around the town are reputed to produce the best orange juice in the Mediterranean. You could also sample the local orange liqueur, called angel d'or, which is used to flavour some of the cakes found on menus and in Sóller's many tempting bakeries.

(www.jardinesdealfabia.com; April–Oct daily 9.30am–6.30pm, Nov–March Mon–Fri 9.30am–5.30pm, Sat 9.30am–1pm), a baronial mansion with wonderful gardens, which was once the country estate of a Moorish vizier of Pollença. The cisterns, fountains and irrigation channels are a bit neglected, but the flowing water and shaded walks, with turkeys pecking beneath fig trees, and birds singing among exotic plants, are appealing. The house is full of treasures: look out for the huge fourteenth-century oak chair regarded as one of the most important antiques in Mallorca. It's easy to see why the gardens are such a popular (and expensive) wedding destination.

FROM BUNYOLA TO CASTLE D'ALARÓ

A few kilometres past the gardens, a left-hand turn points to **Bunyola**, a peaceful little place that produces excellent olive oil and a bright green herbal liqueur called Palo Tunel. The village church and the town hall both stand on the main square, Sa Plaça, which is shaded by leafy plane trees. It's a lovely drive from here to the tiny village of **Orient**, which has a hotel (plus a few in the nearby area) and several restaurants, and is a favourite base for hikers. The **Castell d'Alaró** ⓮, a ruined fortress built by Jaume I, crowns a massive crag 822m (2,700ft) high.

You can walk up from Orient if you have lots of energy, strong shoes and plenty of drinking water, or drive most of the way to the summit up narrow, tortuous lanes, starting a little north of the nearby town of **Alaró**. The tracks get progressively rougher, however, and the final stretch is only suitable for 4WD vehicles. Park before this section begins, at the restaurant *Es Verger*, and look for a sign saying 'Castell a Peu' (To the castle on foot).

That leaves a thirty- to forty-minute climb to reach the summit, not advisable in the sweltering heat of high summer. The views from the top are spectacular, however, and well worth the exertion.

There is a small restaurant and simple, unassuming accommodation, which must be booked in advance (tel: 971 182 112; www.caminsdepedra.conselldemallorca.cat; open year round).

THE HEART OF THE TRAMUNTANA

If you head in the opposite direction from Sóller, towards Pollença, the magnificent views continue as the road cuts through the heart of the Unesco World Heritage-listed Serra de Tramuntana, with **Puig Major** – Mallorca's highest mountain at 1,445m (4,741ft) – looming high above.

Fornalutx ⓯ is an exquisite little town of warm stone buildings that's been designated a national monument – which naturally means it draws in a lot of visitors, but also means building regulations are stringent. Set against the backdrop of the Tramuntana

Fornalutx has been designated a national monument

range, its steep, cobbled streets are lined with cacti and palm trees. A high proportion of the well-restored medieval properties belongs to overseas investors, attracted by the region's beauty. The town is set among ancient terraces of citrus fruits and silver-leaved olive trees, marked out with dry-stone walls. Paths run through them to pretty little **Biniaraix**, which is also only a half-hour walk down narrow lanes, signposted from the centre of Sóller.

A short distance past Fornalutx on the Ma-10, the **Mirador de Ses Barques** has a restaurant where you can stop for a drink while enjoying spectacular views of Port de Sóller and the coast. The route then winds past the reservoirs of Panta de Cúber and Panta de GorgBlau, connected by a narrow canal. Near the latter, a little road leads down to the coast at **Sa Calobra** ⑯. This is one of the most dramatic roads on the island, a serpentine 12km (8 miles) route of near-continuous hairpin bends that zigzag down to sea level. The views are stunning, and the road is an adventure in itself, but try to come early in the morning to avoid the streams of tourist coaches.

Park where you can when the road reaches sea level, and walk a short distance towards the deep gorge of **Torrent de Pareis**. Tunnels burrow through the rock to the riverbed, where the gorge widens into a huge natural amphitheatre. Be extra careful if it has rained, even only a little, as the rocks get very slippery. The idyllic little bay, **Cala de Sa Calobra**, has a couple of waterfront restaurants and bars and a dinky, pebbly beach, but they get very crowded in summer.

MONESTIR DE LLUC

Around 10km (6 miles) further along the road to Pollença is the major pilgrimage site in Mallorca, the **Monestir de Lluc** ⑰ (tel: 971 871 525; www.lluc.net; daily 10am–6.30pm, free; museum Sun–Fri 10am–2pm). Located in a valley near Puig des Castellot,

Cycling near Sa Calobra

the massive abode mainly dates from the eighteenth century, but pilgrims have been coming here since the thirteenth century to pray to a dark-stone statue of the Madonna and Child, La Moreneta. According to legend, it was discovered by an Arab boy called Lluc, whose family had converted to Christianity. He took the statue to the church of Sant Pere in the tiny village of Escorça nearby, but it kept returning to the place where he had found it, so it was finally allowed to stay, and a chapel was built to house it.

People still come to venerate La Moreneta, but many also come to have lunch and admire the views, as the monastery has a restaurant, bar and barbecue area. It also offers inexpensive accommodation; the rooms are pretty basic, but staying here allows you to appreciate the peace of the monastery once the tour groups have gone home. If you attend Mass in the church during the school year, you will have the pleasure of hearing the Lluc boys' and girls' choir, **Els Blavets** (Blue Ones), named after the colour of their cassocks. They also sing in the evenings, on Sundays and at special services.

THE NORTH AND NORTHEAST

The north is a region of great variety. It encompasses the rugged Cap de Formentor, the sandy coves of Sant Vicenç, two attractive towns – Pollença and Alcúdia – the resort of Port de Pollença and the huge, curved Badia d'Alcúdia, lined with resorts and facilities. Parallel to the bay is a complete contrast in the wetlands of the Parc Natural de S'Albufera.

From Palma, it is a fast drive up the Ma-13 motorway to the Ma-2200 turning to Pollença. If continuing the previous route, the road from Lluc curves through holm oak forests before descending to the Vall de Son Marc and Pollença.

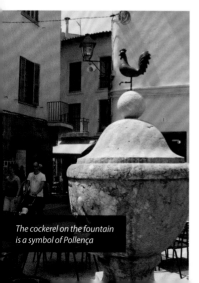

The cockerel on the fountain is a symbol of Pollença

POLLENÇA

Pollença ⓲ has a long history. The Romans may have established a small settlement here (see page 66), and the stone bridge to the north of the town centre is believed to have been built by them, though the actual origin of the bridge is still up for some debate. The Catalan community was founded in 1236 after the Moors were expelled. Present-day Pollença was first shown on a map in 1789; it was a prosperous town, for a while the feudal property of the Knights Templar, and able to support the numerous impressive churches still standing.

Pollença is a lively place, especially during summer evenings, when it teems with visitors; the comings and goings in the Plaça Major provide free entertainment for people sipping cool drinks outside buzzy cafés and restaurants. The *plaça* also comes into its own on Sunday morning (8am–1.30pm), when locals shop for fresh produce in the market, then drink coffee outside *Café Espanyol* (also called *Ca'n Moixet*), after attending Mass in the parochial church, La Mare de Déu des Àngels.

The Carrer de Monte-Sion, leading off the square towards the Jesuit church of the same name, has some great little shops and a clutch of restaurants. Ceramics can be found in *Ceràmiques Monti-Sion*, which offers an excellent range of handcrafted pieces in both traditional and modern designs. Nearby is little Plaça de l'Almoina; the fountain has a cockerel on top, the symbol of the town. In Carrer Roca, the **Fundació i Casa Museu Dionís Bennassar** (www.museudionisbennassar.com; Tues–Fri 10am–3pm, Sat & Sun 10am–2pm) displays the work and personal possessions of this local artist (1904–67) in his family home.

From the parish church in the *plaça* (or from the Ajuntament, off to the left), the Via Crucis (Way of the Cross), a long, calf-punishing flight of 365 steps lined with cypress trees, leads to El Calvari. This little chapel has been given a rhyming name – La Mare de Déu del Peu de la Creu (Mother of God at the Foot of the Cross) – after a fourteenth-century sculpture inside showing Mary at the feet of Christ. At the bottom of the steps is the Museu Martí Vicenç (www.martivicens.org), which exhibits the works of the local artist, sculptor and textile designer.

Back in town, the deconsecrated Dominican convent and church of **Sant Domingo** (summer Mon–Fri 9am–4pm, Sun

10am–1pm, winter Mon–Fri 8am–3pm; free) is now a temple to culture rather than worship. Exhibitions of installation art are staged in the nave of the great seventeenth-century church in summer, and the cloisters are the venue for a classical music festival in July or August (see page 95), when an international line-up of orchestras and soloists performs. Pollença's **Museu Municipal** (winter Tues–Sun 11am–1pm, summer Tues–Sat 10am–1pm & 5.30–8.30pm) is also housed inside the monastery in a large, light space. Somewhat eclectic, it includes changing exhibitions of contemporary paintings and sculpture, a permanent collection of Gothic art, some early twentieth-century paintings and a few archaeological finds.

Outside the convent, the **Jardins Joan March Severa**, built around a watchtower and an antique water wheel, has an interesting collection of Balearic plants. The garden is always open, but the

PUIG DE SANTA MARIA

Just outside Pollença on the Palma road is a path up to the **Santuari del Puig**, the medieval convent on top of the 330m-high (1,083ft) Puig de Santa Maria. The first half of the 4km (2-mile) trail can be tackled by car if you have nerves of steel; the latter part only on foot. The dry-stone walls (*margers*) along the last section are a good demonstration of an ancient skill that is now dying out. The views from the top, stretching as far as the Serra de Tramuntana, Cap de Formentor, the plain of Sa Pobla and the bays of Alcúdia and Pollença, are superb. The fourteenth-century Gothic convent began as a plea for protection against the Black Death, but quickly became one of the most sacred buildings on the island. Accommodation is available and there is a bar and a restaurant (prior notice needed for accommodation, tel: 971 184 132).

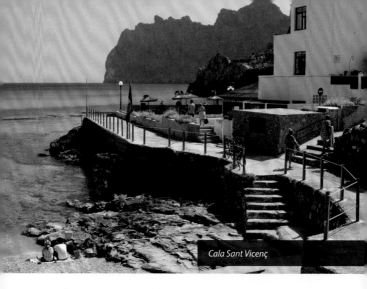
Cala Sant Vicenç

watchtower is not accessible. Carrer Roser Vell leads off to the left; at its far end you will see the plain facade of the little fourteenth-century oratory of **Roser Vell**.

CALA SANT VICENÇ AND PORT DE POLLENÇA

About 3km (2 miles) along the Ma-2200 from Pollença to its port is the turning to **Cala Sant Vicenç** ⓳, a family resort built around three sandy coves with brilliant blue water, excellent for swimming and snorkelling – although strong winds can whip up quite quickly.

A couple more kilometres along the main road brings you to **Port de Pollença**. Tucked into the wide curve of a bay, with the marina in the centre, it has been popular with English visitors for many years and retains a distinctive atmosphere. However, it is a resort with an alter-ego. To the north of the marina, the prom-enade has a plethora of restaurants, some with tables spilling

Hermen Camarasa

On the promenade north of the marina, you may notice a memorial bust of Hermen Anglada Camarasa (1872–1959), the Catalan *Moderniste* painter after whom this stretch is named. He lived and worked in Pollença for many years. A collection of his work can be seen in the CaixaForum in the old *Gran Hotel* in Palma (see page 35).

onto the sands, and a couple of stylish hotels. These give way to old, one-storey houses and wooden jetties, where the branches of trees almost reach the water.

To the south of the marina, however, the palm-shaded promenade that flanks the lovely, long sweep of sandy beach is lined wall-to-wall with cheap and cheerful tripper shops and fast-food joints. The narrow streets unfurling from behind the northerly promenade are nicer. There's a lot to do, though: sailing and scuba lessons are on offer, and there are boat trips to Formentor and Cala Sant Vicenç.

CAP DE FORMENTOR

Continuing round the bay to the southeast, towards Alcúdia, the commercial zone ends abruptly, and the beach narrows to a sliver, popular with windsurfers, with an isolated expanse of lonely wetlands on the other side.

But before heading in this direction, make a trip to the island's northernmost point, **Cap de Formentor ⓴**, the slender headland on the north side of the Badia de Pollença. With sheer cliffs and an idyllic sandy beach, the rocky peninsula, caressed by clear turquoise waters, is simply spectacular. The best place to appreciate the extraordinary landscape is the **Mirador de la Creueta**, about 5km (3 miles) from Port de Pollença, where there is a specially designed walkway to make the most of this vantage point. Some tour buses don't trudge any further than this, which is a blessing for motorists, as the twisting road is a challenging one, demanding much concentration, and can get swamped with traffic in summer.

Just beyond the Mirador de la Creueta, the pretty, pine-shaded beach (signposted Platja de Formentor on the right-hand side), is a favourite spot for a picnic and offers splendid views across the bay – similar to those you would get from the exclusive *Hotel Formentor*, which was recently snapped up by the Four Seasons Group for a scheduled reopening in 2023. The hotel was built in 1928 by an Argentinian architect, Adam Diehl, and quickly became popular with a fashionable set, which included the Duke of Windsor and Mrs Simpson, Sir Winston Churchill and the Rainiers of Monaco.

Cap de Formentor

From the beach turn-off, it's another 12km (8 miles) to the lighthouse at the tip. Just before you enter the tunnel that leads through El Fumat, there's a great view of the sparkling waters of the Badia de Pollença glistening far below.

ALCÚDIA

Retrace your steps past Port de Pollença to the ancient, walled town of **Alcúdia ㉑**. There were Phoenician and Greek settlements here before the Romans founded their city in 123BC, and called it Pollentia. The Vandals sacked it, the Moors rebuilt it – Al Kudia (means 'on the hill') – and the conquering Spaniards fortified it in the thirteenth century. The sturdy walls and gates now standing are later imitations, but still impressive. Today, it's an inviting, unpretentious little place, with some excellent Renaissance facades;

Alfresco dining in Alcúdia

good cafés and restaurants on the central **Plaça Constitució**; and a lively market on Tuesdays and Sundays (8am–1.30pm), held just outside the city walls.

The sturdy neo-Gothic church of **Sant Jaume**, which has a lovely rose window and Baroque altars, forms the southern bastion in the walls. Opposite the church, in a small, fourteenth-century building, is the Museo Monogràfic de Pollentia (summer Mon–Fri 9.30am–8.30pm, Sat & Sun 9.30am–2.30pm, winter Tues–Sat 10am–3pm). It has an extensive collection of Roman finds, including ceramics, glassware, tools and surgical instruments. You can pick up a free leaflet here, describing points of interest in the Roman city. The remains of that city, the **Ciutat Romana del Pollentia** (hours as above), excavated in the 1950s by members of a dig organized by American archaeologist William Bryant, stand outside the walls (there's a large carpark, and a bus from Palma stops nearby). The area includes remnants of a string of buildings, and gives a good idea of the town's layout. The star turn, however, is the substantial remains of the Teatre Romà (Roman Theatre), dating from the first century BC.

PORT D'ALCÚDIA AND THE BAY

Port d'Alcúdia has evolved from a small fishing harbour into an all-purpose port for commercial, naval and pleasure craft, and is one of the largest resorts on the north coast. Restaurants, cafés and clubs have mushroomed rapidly, as have high-rise hotels and apartment blocks, which now spread around the bay to form an almost unbroken ribbon of buildings 10km (6 miles) long.

To the east of the port, on a wide and rocky headland, is the Museu Sa Bassa Blanca, formerly the Fundació Yannick y Ben Jakober (www.msbb.org; times vary – consult website), which displays portraits of children from the sixteenth to the nineteenth centuries. There is also a collection of contemporary art and a sculpture park.

In summer, the stretch of glorious white sand beaches abutting **Port d'Alcúdia** is a mass of bodies soaking up the sun's rays or sheltering beneath colourful umbrellas. Although big, crowded and impersonal, the resort, which more or less merges into Ca'n Picafort at the eastern end, does not have the seediness of some of the southern spots. Both remain low-key, if perhaps a bit soulless, and are good options for families with children or teenagers in need of entertainment.

As you drive along the main road, lined with supermarkets, shops and high-rise hotels, signs saying simply 'Platja' lead to the beach. The area around **Platja de Muro** is a bit quieter, but not by much.

PARC NATURAL DE S'ALBUFERA

About halfway between Port d'Alcúdia and Can Picafort, almost opposite the *Hotel Parc Natural* (www.grupotel.com), is the entrance to the **Parc Natural de S'Albufera** ㉒ (daily April–Sept 9am–6pm, Oct–March 9am–5pm; free). There's a carpark a few metres further along from the entrance. It seems remarkable to find this huge swathe of wetlands so close to major resorts, and it can be a real haven for visitors as well as for birds, more than 200 species of which have been spotted here. A free permit must be picked up from the Reception Centre, about 1km (0.5 miles) from the entrance (9am–4pm). The reserve sprawls across 800 hectares (2,000 acres), with walking and cycling tracks through it, and is crisscrossed by a network of canals constructed in the nineteenth century by a British company that began reclaiming marshland for agriculture, but ran out of money. The area became a protected zone in 1988, one of the first beneficiaries of the new environmental consciousness.

ES PLA, OR THE PLAIN

Bounded by mountains and hills to the north and east, the central portion of Mallorca is called **Es Pla** (The Plain). Lightly populated and not particularly geared towards visitors, there are lovely agricultural landscapes with ancient stone farmhouses (*fincas*), olive groves and unassuming old towns. The region is known as 'the land of a thousand windmills' and, while it's unlikely that anyone has counted, there certainly are a lot of them. They are a landmark of the island, and many have been restored and put back into use, particularly around Sa Pobla.

The land of a thousand windmills

This route starts at Pollença and swings by several inland towns, with a detour to Randa, the 'monastery mountain', but narrow country roads run off in all directions and can be worth exploring.

SA POBLA

The Ma-2200 runs about 12km (8 miles) through fertile farmland to **Sa Pobla**, an unexceptional but pleasant town with fine old buildings clustered around the main square and a church consecrated to Sant Antoni Abat. The Sunday-morning food market is worth a visit, and a jazz festival takes place in Sa Pobla throughout August.

From here, you can continue down the main Ma-13 to Inca. It is not a particularly interesting town, but it is worth a visit for its

Festival of Pets

On 16 January, a popular festival in honour of Sant Antoni Abat is celebrated in Sa Pobla, with an enormous bonfire, music and the eating of *espinagades* (pastries filled with spiced vegetables and S'Albufera eel). The next day, the town's more amenable pets are led in a street procession and then blessed outside the church.

cellers (see page 72) and for the factory shop selling Camper shoes.

BINISSALEM AND SINEU

Binissalem, located around 8km (5 miles) further down the main road, is the heart of the wine-producing district. You will see silvery vineyards stretching for miles around – particularly attractive in late summer, when plump grapes are nearly ready for picking. There's a wine festival here every September celebrating the bounty of the vines.

It's better, though, to take the rural (but good) road to **Sineu** ㉓, at the centre of the island, the pick of the inland towns. It has an elegant Gothic church, with some lovely reliefs by the Mannerist Gaspar Gener (1563–90), a Baroque retable and some interesting modern stained glass.

There is also a handful of attractive Renaissance mansions in the town, and a peaceful plaza with good restaurants. Its Wednesday-morning market (typically 8am–2pm) is the most authentic on the island.

FROM PETRA TO THE SANCTUARIES

From Sineu, it is about 11km (6 miles) to **Petra** ㉔. One reason people go to this sleepy little town is to visit the Casa Museu Fray Juníper Serra (www.fundacioncasaserra.org; Tues–Sat 9.30am–1.30pm; tel: 971 561 028 or book at www.spiritualmallorca.com).

Petra is the birthplace of Fray Serra (1713–84); one of Mallorca's best-known sons, he was a Franciscan monk who founded numerous missions in California and was canonized by Pope Francis in 2015 – no matter the devastating effects the missions (and European diseases) had on the Indigenous population. The museum, run by a dedicated Society of Friends, illustrates these and other missions; his house next door is more interesting, a modest place with cell-like rooms and a pretty garden. Wall tiles on the usually closed monastery of Sant Bernardino, opposite, depict the Californian missions; and signs lead to *Es Celler* (see page 72).

From Petra, it is less than 5km (3 miles) on the Ma-3320 to the main Palma road (MA-15). The first town en route in the direction of Palma is Vilafranca de Bonany, known for the production of sweet little tomatoes, garlic, red peppers and melons. A little further along, a turning on the right takes you to Els Calderers de Sant Joan (daily April–Oct 10am–6pm, Nov–March 10am–5pm; www.elscalderers.com), an eighteenth-century manor house with a chapel, a granary and an extensive estate and farm. You can sample home-made products as part of the tour.

Still heading towards Palma, turn off at Algaida to visit Puig de Randa, the highest point on Es Pla at

Colourful shutters in Sineu

543m (1,781ft), crowned by the **Santuari de Nostra Senyora de Cura** ㉕ (tel: 971 120 260; www.santuaridecura.com; museum and church hours summer 10am–1.30pm & 3pm–6pm, winter 10am–1.30pm & 3pm–5pm), which has accommodation and a bar-restaurant. The philosopher and mystic Ramón Llull (1235–1316) established the original sanctuary.

On your way up to the hilltop church, you pass the Oratori de Gràcia and the hermitage of Sant Honorat. Randa is the centre of a little cluster of sanctuaries. Not far away, the Ermita de la Pau has a Romanesque chapel; and, just above the village of Porreres, you can drive the 4km (2.5 miles) up to the Santuari de Monte-Sión, which contains a fifteenth-century marble statue of the Verge de Monte-Sión.

To return to Palma, continue on the Ma-15 or get onto the motorway (MA-19) at Llucmajor. For the east coast, take the Ma-15 towards Manacor, then north to Artà.

CULINARY CELLERS

Anyone interested in the true *cuina Mallorquina* – Mallorcan cooking – should visit a *celler*. These cool basement bodegas were originally wine shops and are still lined with huge oak barrels, but have now become restaurants, serving large helpings of island food. They exist all over the island, but there are some especially renowned ones in the inland towns. Inca has about half a dozen, of which *Can Amer* (www.celler-canamer.es) is the best known. In Sineu, the *Cellar Ca'n Font* on the main square is the place to go, while the best one in Petra is *Es Celler* (www.restaurantsceller.com)(see page 112 for details). They won't suit anyone who wants to eat outside in the sun, but their cavernous depths can be refreshing on a hot day.

THE EAST AND SOUTHEAST

Most of the bays and beaches along the east coast have become overdeveloped and overcrowded, but the resorts are nicer and far less excessive than those around the Bay of Palma, and some spots – harbours such as Port Colom and Cala Figuera – are still delightful. There are also two fortified towns in the northeast corner – Artà and Capdepera –

Cruising off Cala Mesquida

and a string of amazing caves to visit, plus the prehistoric sites of Ses Païsses (near Artà) and Capocorp Vell, near the south coast.

ARTÀ AND SES PAÏSSES

Artà ㉖ lies 12km (8 miles) inland, a fortified town that has retained a friendly, everyday atmosphere, and not become a mere showcase for its historic sites. It has a handful of decent hotels with restaurants (see pages 112 and 141), and is a good place to stay if you want to escape the crowded resorts of the coast.

In a palazzo on the Plaça d'Espanya, the recently renovated **Museu Regional d'Artà** (www.museuarta.com; Tues–Sat 10am–2pm) rubs shoulders with the town hall and has a series of archaeological finds dating from the Phoenician, Greek and Roman periods, as well as a natural science collection.

The ancient church of the **Sant Salvador**, with a large rose window above the main portal, is one of Artà's major sites. Beyond, the Via Crucis (Way of the Cross), a broad flight of steps flanked by cypress trees and stone crosses, leads to the Santuari de Sant Salvador d'Artà. Construction started in the thirteenth century on the remains of a Moorish structure and, today, you can walk along the walls of this shrine, providing splendid views across the plain to the coast. You may be lucky and arrive while a recital is being given in the church – a wonderful experience.

The prehistoric settlement of **Ses Païsses** ㉗ (Mon–Fri 10am–5pm, Sat 10am–2pm) is about 2km (1 mile) southeast of Artà on the Cami Corballa. A path leads from the shady carpark through an impressive gateway in the Cyclopean wall wrapping around the settlement. The ruins, concealed among holm oaks, include square foundations, a *talayot* (watch tower) with a small chamber at its base, and an oval chamber with the remains of several pillars.

CAPDEPERA

Barely 8km (5 miles) east of Artà is the ochre-coloured town of **Capdepera**, its streets filled with flowers. Steps lead from the Plaça d'Espanya to the **Castell de Capdepera** (www.castellcapdepera.com; daily mid-March to mid-Oct 10am–10pm, mid-Oct to mid-Mar 9am–5pm). One of the best-preserved castles in Mallorca, it originated in Roman times, was enlarged by the Moors and strengthened further by the

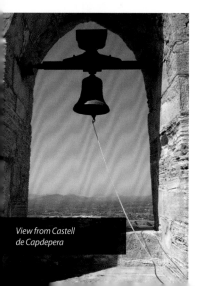

View from Castell de Capdepera

Christians. Beneath the defensive wall, from which there is a superb view, stands the nineteenth-century church of Sant Bartomeu.

From Capdepera, a road runs through farmland, past the Canyamel Golf Club (www.canyamelgolf.com), where a new road layout nods at impending urbanization, then winds high above the Platja Canyamel development to the **Coves d'Artà** ㉘ (daily April–June & Oct 10am–6pm, July–Sept until 7pm, Nov–March until 5pm; guided tours in English last around 35–40 mins). Carved out of the sheer cliff face, the caves are less commercialized than the Coves del Drac (see page 76), and the limestone rock formations are quite awesome. In the summer, you can hop on a boat here from Cala Ratjada.

CALA RATJADA

It is only 3km (2 miles) from Capdepera to **Cala Ratjada** (also spelled Rajada), a busy resort built on a grid pattern. It was once the most important fishing harbour on the island, after Palma, but much of the port is now used for leisure, as you can see from the boats moored here. There is an abundance of accommodation, although much of it is prebooked by tour companies; and a rash of fast-food outlets and tourist-tat shops can detract from the atmosphere. However, much of the seafront is attractive, with restaurant tables set among pines and succulents. There is one sandy beach in the centre of town, where good waves attract surfboarders, but most people head to the beaches a little further north. The northernmost one is **Cala Agulla**, with beautiful, protected dunes.

The **Platja de Son Moll** to the south of the resort can be reached via the promenade. Still further south is **Sa Font de Sa Cala**, named after a freshwater spring that flows directly into the sea. Here, a lovely little beach has been completely overwhelmed by two huge hotel complexes.

Up, up and away

A unique way to see the island is from the air. Mallorca Balloons (Carrer Farallo 4, Cala Ratjada; tel: 971 596 969; www.mallorcaballoons. com) offers several different flights, including trips over the Serra de Tramuntana mountains, moonlight flights, breakfast flights and trips to see the almond blossom in bloom.

On a hill above Cala Ratjada's harbour, the **Sa Torre Cega** can only be visited by prior reservation (tel: 971 711 122 ; www.fundacionbmarch.es), but the impressive modern sculpture displayed there makes it worth the effort.

CALA MILLOR TO PORTO CRISTO

The next resort complex, the largest and loudest on the east coast, is **Cala Millor**, where three separate *calas* merge together along the sandy beach of Son Severa. The resort is still growing, and the neighbouring promontory of **Punta de N'Amer**, a 200-hectare (495-acre) nature reserve, is the only area that has swerved development.

The road south passes the Safari-Zoo (see page 96) before reaching **Porto Cristo**, an old-fashioned resort with a pleasant, local atmosphere. There is a large yacht marina, an unremarkable beach and a couple of traditional hotels vying with modern buildings. It's popular with Mallorcan visitors at weekends, when the narrow streets can get clogged.

Most of the tour buses here are shuttling visitors to the **Coves del Drac** ㉙ (www.cuevasdeldrach.com; daily mid-March to Oct 10am–5pm, Nov to mid-March 10.45am–3.30pm), south of town. Seven daily tours in summer (four in winter) run through 2km (1 mile) of brightly lit chambers and spectacular formations, culminating with classical music recitals and boat trips on the 177m (581ft)-long subterranean lake named after

Edouard-Alfred Martel, the French speleologist who explored the caves in 1896.

On the road to Manacor, the Coves dels Hams (www.cuevas-delshams.com; daily end March to June 10am–5pm, July–29 Oct 10am–5pm, 30 Oct–15 Nov 10am–4.30pm, mid-Nov to March 10am–4pm) are competing for subterranean custom by offering a digital 'virtual adventure'.

FELANITX AND THE SANTUARI DE SANT SALVADOR

It's a pleasant drive south through agricultural land, with minor roads darting off to beaches. To the right, just before Porto Colom, is **Felanitx** – you will see watchtowers on the hill as you approach. This was the birthplace, in 1957, of the painter Miquel Barceló, and it is a good place to buy ceramics. There is a lively market on Sunday morning, and an impressive, partly thirteenth-century church, Sant Miquel.

En route to Felanitx, turn off to the **Santuari de Sant Salvador** ③, 509m (1,670ft) above sea level. The first sanctuary here was built in 1348; today's structure dates from 1734. On one side of the hill is a 14m (46ft) stone cross, and on the other, the monument to Cristo Rei (Christ the King). The monastery church contains a fine alabaster retable

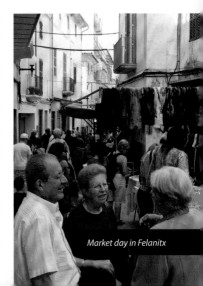

Market day in Felanitx

Cala Mondragó

showing scenes from *The Last Supper*. There is also a display of championship cyclists' jerseys, fading in glass cases along with notes of homage to the virgin. You can drive right up to the sanctuary. There are magnificent views, and accommodation in the *Petit Hotel Hostatgería Sant Salvador* (tel: 971 515 260; www.santsalvadorhotel.com), with a clutch of bright, airy guest rooms and a good restaurant.

PORTO COLOM TO CALA MONDRAGÓ

Reached on the Ma-4010 from Felanitx, **Porto Colom** is still a working fishing port, where you can watch the daily catch brought ashore. There is a strip of beach along the bay, but the lack of a significant, sandy swathe has ensured that Porto Colom remains a pleasant place, with a pine-shaded promenade and some pretty, pastel-coloured houses. Holiday apartments line the streets inland, but the only real commercial development is around the bay at Cala Marçal, south of the harbour.

Cala d'Or is only 7km (4 miles) further south, but you have to swerve inland then return to the coast. A resort of many years standing, it has evolved into a huge, sometimes stylish, complex taking in a necklace of coves and beaches. The architecture is homogeneous – low-rise, flat-roofed and often bright white. The coves are pretty, and the swimming is good; the harbour plays host to some elegant yachts, and there are all the tourist facilities and watersports you could want.

If you want to escape it all, you must continue a little further south to Porto Petro, an attractive harbour with a yacht club and some decent restaurants; then wend your way to **Cala Mondragó**, which is off the beaten track and practically undeveloped in comparison with most of the coast. It should stay that way, because the two miniscule sandy beaches are part of the 785-hectare (1,940-acre) **Parc Natural Mondragó ③** (information centre in the carpark; daily 9am–4pm; free), which also encompasses farmland and wetlands. Walking tracks weave through the park, offering plentiful opportunities to birdwatch and look for the wild orchids growing beneath the trees. A couple of hotels and beach restaurants are here, but it's all very low-key.

SANTANYÍ AND CALA FIGUERA

Return to the main road and, after 5km (3 miles), you'll reach **Santanyí ㉜**, a mellow little town of honey-coloured sandstone and one gate, Sa Porta Murada, remaining from the fortified walls. The elongated Plaça Major is edged by friendly cafés, but is dominated by the huge fortified church of Sant Andreu Apostol, which has a famously ornate organ and incorporates the Gothic gems of the Capella del Roser, a survivor from the first church built on the site. There's an arty feel to Santanyí, with a gaggle of exhibition venues, and rows of antiques and ceramics shops.

Cala Figuera ㉝ is delightful, a fishing port with neat green-and-white houses and a walkway flanked by boathouses right at the water's edge. A handful of yachts bob in the waters, but they do not outnumber or outshine the working vessels. There are plenty of restaurants and some accommodation, but the tourist industry has not grown out of hand.

Cala Figuera

JOURNEY'S END

Back to the main road again, and the first stop after Santanyí is **Botanicactus** ❸ (www.botanicactus. com; daily April–Aug 9am–7.30pm, Sept–Oct till 7pm, Nov–Feb 10.30am–4.30pm, March 9am–6.30pm). This is one of the better botanical gardens in the Balearics, and contains 1500 different plant species. It's not all cacti – there's an artificial lake surrounded by palms, and an assortment of indigenous flowers. Some 7km (4 miles) away is Colònia de Sant Jordi, one of Mallorca's earliest resorts. Its pleasant harbour is the starting point for trips to Cabrera, and you can walk around the dunes to the south of the bay. To the west of Sant Jordi, the sandy stretch of **Platja Es Trenc** is now a protected area, so major development will not be permitted.

The main road west from Santanyí, through a flat, agricultural landscape where many of the windmills have been renovated with brightly coloured sails, leads to **Campos** ❸, an agricultural town with two huge, sandstone churches. The Església Parroquial Sant Julià contains a painting by Murillo (1617–82), but it is usually only open for mass.

The road then heads to Llucmajor, an ancient town with a smattering of striking *Moderniste* buildings. If you want to head straight to Palma, the new stretch of motorway will take you almost the whole way. Otherwise, follow signs to **Capocorb Vell**

36 (www.talaiotscapocorbvell.com; Fri–Wed 10am–5pm), one of the better-known prehistoric sites in Mallorca. The remaining foundations of twenty-eight enormous buildings can be seen, and at the edge of the settlement are a pair of imposing *talayots* and three round towers.

You can drop down to **Cap Blanc 37**, where a lighthouse rises above a rugged, rocky promontory. From here, the road runs along a rather dull stretch of coast towards the Platja de Palma. S'Arenal, the largest resort, merges into Les Meravelles on a 7km (4-mile) strip of packed beaches, fast-food outlets, high-rise hotels, high-throttle clubs, English pubs, Murphy's bars and German beer halls.

Approaching the yacht harbour of Ca'n Pastilla, the road becomes pedestrianized and more inviting – and then you are back in Palma.

CABRERA: A NATURAL PARADISE

Cabrera, an uninhabited island cast adrift 17km (10 miles) south of Cap de Ses Salines, has been protected as a nature reserve since 1991. In season, it's easily visited on a boat trip from Colònia de Sant Jordi (www.excursionsacabrera.es), but otherwise – if you are travelling there independently – you will need permission to visit; www.reservasparquesnacionales.es. It is only 7km (4 miles) by 5km (3 miles) in size, with a rocky coast giving way to rugged limestone interior, where a track leads 72m (236ft) up to the castle. There is a pair of dinky bays, good for swimming and snorkelling. Bring your own supplies, or opt for lunch on a tour boat, because there is no-where to buy food or water. During the Napoleonic Wars, Cabrera was used to house French prisoners, and it was later garrisoned by the Spanish army.

Mallorca is a sailing paradise

THINGS TO DO

SPORTS

Most outdoor activities in Mallorca revolve around the ocean and there is a huge range of things to do, including sailing, wind-surfing, kitesurfing, paragliding, water-skiing, paddle boarding, snorkelling, fishing and, of course, swimming. However, walking, climbing and birdwatching are catching up in popularity, drawing thousands of visitors to the island, especially in spring and autumn, when the mild weather makes hiking a pleasure, and numerous species of migrating birds enthral birdwatchers. Mallorca is also a great place for cycling, horse riding and golf.

SAILING

The Balearics are a sailing paradise. British Olympic gold medallist sailor Sir Ben Ainslie is, for one, very partial to the area. The island has a wealth of safe harbours and over thirty marinas, and thousands of foreign visitors moor boats here year round.

You can hire various kinds of craft for an hour, a day or week at many beaches and hotels. The Asociación Provincial de Empresarios de Actividades Marítimas de Baleares is the biggest yacht charter company (tel: 971 727 986; www.apeam.com). The Centro Náutico Port de Sóller, Platja d'En Repic, Port de Sóller (tel: 609 354 132; www.nauticsoller.com), is recommended for boat or kayak hire and organizes water-based excursions. The Escuela Nacional de Vela Calanova, Avinguda Joan Miró 327, Palma (tel: 971 402 512), offers intensive beginners' courses; as does Centro Náutico Port de Sóller. Sail and Surf Pollença, Passeig Saralegui, Port de Pollença (tel: 971 865 346; www.sailsurf.de) is a prestigious club that offers instruction for beginners and more advanced sailors.

Windsurfing is popular in Mallorca

WINDSURFING AND WATER-SKIING

There are windsurfing schools, with equipment hire, at several of the larger resorts. Sail and Surf Pollença offers windsurf hire and tuition, as does Water Sports Mallorca (tel: 606 353 807; www.watersportsmallorca.com), which has a school in Alcúdia offering windsurfing, kitesurfing, surfing and catamaran classes. Also in Alcúdia is Spain's longest cable ski for wakeboarders (tel: 633 664 439; www.mallorcawakepark.com). On the east coast, windsurfing facilities are available at Cala Millor and Cala d'Or. Water-skiing equipment can be hired on many beaches, including Cala Millor, Can Picafort and Port d'Alcúdia.

SCUBA DIVING

Easily the best spot for scuba diving on Mallorca are the clear and reefy waters in the southwest corner of the island, off Sant Elm. Here and elsewhere, scuba-diving equipment is available for hire if you have a qualification from your home country. The Federación Balear de Actividades Subacuaticas, Carrer de l'Uruguai, 07010 Palma, Illes Balears (tel: 971 708 785; www.fbdas. com), can give information and advice. The numerous scuba-diving clubs include two in the southwestern corner: Dragonera Dives (Aqua Marine Diving), Port d'Andratx (tel: 971 674 376; www.aqua-mallorca-diving.com), and Scuba Activa, Sant Elm (tel: 971 239 102; www.scuba-activa.com). There's also Big Blue Diving, in Palmanova (tel: 971 681 686; www.bigbluediving.net), with numerous sites for people of all ability levels, and in Port de Pollença, there's Scuba Mallorca (tel: 971 868 087; www. scubamallorca.com).

BOAT TRIPS

Boat trips are available from several points along the west coast. In Port de Sóller, Barcos Azules, Muelle comercial, S/N Local 2-3 (tel: 971 630 170; www.barcos-calobra.com), runs a variety of trips around the rugged coast and tiny bays, including cruises to Sa Calobra. Boat trips operate from most ports, some using glass-bottomed boats.

WALKING AND CLIMBING

The Mallorcan landscape is perfect for dedicated

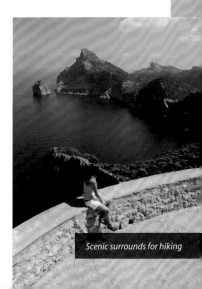

Scenic surrounds for hiking

There are serious rocks in Mallorca for climbers

hikers and more leisurely walkers. April and May, when the island is carpeted in wildflowers, are the best months, while September and October are good, too. In the hotter seasons, start early in the day or make use of the long evenings. Needless to say, correct footwear is essential, and common sense will tell you that a supply of water, a wide-brimmed hat and sunscreen are wise precautions.

The **Serra de Tramuntana** makes for the most dramatic scenery, for example, on the dramatic climb up to the Castell d'Alaró (see page 56) and between the Monestir de Lluc and the Cuber reservoir. In the southeast corner, a tangle of walking trails unfurls through the pine groves, marshlands and dunes of the **Parc Natural de Mondragó** (information office open daily 9am–4pm; www.balearsnatura.com). These are on flatter and more gentle paths than those in the northwest. The tourist office in Sóller (tel: 971 638 008) produces a leaflet outlining walking excursions in the immediate vicinity. Walkers' maps are widely available in local bookshops and newsagents. In addition, the website www.camins-mallorca.info has lots of information. The best guided walks are organized by the small and independent Mallorcan Walking Tours (www.mallorcanwalkingtours.com).

There are also serious rocks in Mallorca for climbers. Contact the Federació Balear de Muntanyisme (www.fbmweb.com) or Grup

Excursionista de Mallorca (www.gemweb.org; website in Catalan only). Rocksport Mallorca (tel: 629 948 404; www.facebook.com/RocksportMallorca) offers courses for all levels.

GOLF

There are over twenty 18-hole golf courses in Mallorca, and some are challenging enough for even the best players. You can also hire equipment and take lessons. The carefully landscaped **Arabella Golf** (tel: 971 783 000; www.arabellagolfmallorca.com) hosts a yearly 63-hole Golf Marathon, while the course at **Golf Santa Ponça** (tel: 971 690 211; www.golf-santaponsa.com) is one of Europe's longest.

On the east side of the island, Canyamel (tel: 971 841 313; www.canyamelgolf.com) and Capdepera (tel: 971 818 500; www.golf-capdepera.com) are both popular golf courses. For further information on golfing in Mallorca, check the website of the **Federació Balear de Golf** (www.fbgolf.com).

BIRDWATCHING

Mallorca is one of the most rewarding birdwatching sites in Europe. The island's resident birds are enticing enough, but it's the visiting species that generate most excitement. Migrant birds stop off in spring – as many as 200 species have been spotted – and some stay for the summer. The best birdwatching sites are in the mountainous **Tramuntana** region, where rare black vultures and other birds of prey can be spotted; the **Parc Natural de Mondragó** (www.balearsnatura.com) for marine birds; and the **Parc Natural de S'Albufera** (www.balearsnatura.com) – probably the best wetland site on any Mediterranean island – for the widest variety of all. Head to the birdwatching centre in La Gola (Carrer Temple Fielding; Mon–Sat 8am–1pm; www.ctolagola.com), Port de Pollença for further information.

HORSE RIDING

There is a scattering small ranches and stables across the island, and some *agroturisme* properties offer treks or can arrange them for you. A few of the reputable riding schools are: **Ranxo Ses Roques** (Port d'Alcudia, tel: 971 892 809; www.ranxosesroques.com), **Rancho Jaume** (Porto Petro, tel: 629 627 063; www.rancho-jaume.eu) and **Hípica Formentor** (tel: 609 826 703; www.hipica-formentor.com), which offers treks on well-cared-for rescue horses.

CYCLING

Bikes can be hired at most resorts. Check brakes and tyres, and make sure a lock and puncture kit are included. Ask at the local tourist office for information on cycling routes. In the capital, bikes can be hired by the hour or day at **Palma on Bike**, in the city centre at Av. Antoni Maura 10 (tel: 971 718 062; www.palmaonbike.com); the company also organizes bike tours and rents out rollerblades and kayaks. Always carry ID.

SPECTATOR SPORTS

Football is as popular in Mallorca as in other parts of Spain, and there are dozens of amateur and semi-professional clubs. In 2016, American businessman Robert Sarver purchased **RCD Mallorca** (aka Real Mallorca) and, since then, the team has worked its way back into La Liga. They play at Son Moix stadium at Camí del Rei, Palma (www.rcdmallorca.es). Tickets are usually available to buy on the day.

Bullfights *(corridas)* are still technically legal, but a new law passed by the Balearic parliament in 2017 (following a previous attempt to ban them outright, which was overturned by the Constitutional Court) added rules and regulations that made the 'sport' almost impossible to stage: for one thing, the law forbade the killing of the bulls.

Horse races are held weekly, all year round, at the Hipòdrom de Son Pardo near Palma (www.instituthipicdemallorca.com). Betting is organized through a centralized tote system.

SHOPPING

Shopping in Mallorca is more expensive than it used to be, but you will still find some bargains, particularly if you are looking for leather goods or glass.

Shopping in Pollença

For designer labels, however, **Carrer Verí**, in Palma's old town, has some smart boutiques, as well as a clutch of antique shops; and **Carrer Estanc**, off the Passeig de Born, is lined with chic clothing and interior design shops.

Avinguda Jaume III is the capital's major shopping artery, flanked by big-name clothing shops as well as a huge branch of Spain's biggest department store, El Corte Inglés, which has a supermarket in the basement.

LEATHER

The Balearic Islands are justly famous for their leather industries. Excellent shoes, belts and bags and some of the finest leather and suede jackets come from the islands. The focus of the leather industry is **Inca**, where you can shop at the factory outlets or the local market, though the goods may not be any cheaper than those you will find in Palma.

Books

An extraordinary treasure trove of new and second-hand English books can be found at **Fine Books**, Carrer Morey 7, Palma (tel: 971 723 797): three floors of jumbled volumes, with everything from first editions to nearly new paperbacks, prints and old photos.

If you like shoes, then you'll love shopping in Mallorca. You can go to the factory shop of the quirky shoe company Camper (on the main road around Inca), whose highly individual shoes have become well known. Camper also has outlets in Palma, in Avinguda Jaume III and Carrer Sant Miquel. Less trendy, but extremely attractive and comfortable are *abarcas*, the slipper-like sandals made in Menorca that have been worn by peasants for centuries.

LINEN

Mallorca's embroidered table and bed linens are attractive, and the market in Llucmajor is a great place to find them. Other towns known for good-quality embroidery are Manacor, Pollença and Artà. In Palma, you will see shops selling fine, hand-embroidered linen – and a lot of others selling machine-made versions.

GLASSWARE, POTTERY AND PEARLS

High-quality glassware has been made on the island for centuries. The **Gordiola Museu del Vidre** (www.gordiola.com) factory and museum, outside Algaida on the Palma–Manacor road, is a good place to go. You can watch glass-blowing and see some of the antique pieces on which many current products are based. It also has a showroom in Palma, at Carrer Victoria 2.

Pottery is another traditional craft. There are two main types of cooking pots: *ollas* (round) and *greixeras* (flat and shallow).

Siurells are small, clay whistles painted in red and green, based on Phoenician and Carthaginian originals.

Mallorcan cultured (artificial) pearls, Perlas Majorica, manufactured in Manacor, are exported in huge numbers. One of the best places to buy them is at the (well-signposted) **Orquidea Pearl Factory** (www.pearls-factory.com) on the Ma-15 east of Palma, near Montuiri, where you take a factory tour and have the biggest choice in designs. However, you can buy them all over the island, including Palma at Avinguda Jaume III 15, but while prices don't tend to vary between shops, it's worth noting that they can be pretty expensive.

FOOD AND DRINK

Mallorca is known for its herbal **liqueurs**, and the popular aperitif, palo, is a novelty. One of the most popular brands is Tunel. Look for it in bright green bottles stamped with the train logo, and decide if you want the sweet variety (*dulce*) or the dry (*amargo*). Also worth trying is the orange liqueur, angel d'or, made in Sóller; as is wine from Binissalem, as you are unlikely to find it outside the island. **Olive oil** from around Bunyola is an excellent buy, not cheap but fine quality. Olives, too, are worth taking home. For a selection of Mallorcan varieties, in all

Olives are abundant in Mallorca

shapes, sizes and shades, acquire a plastic container and fill it up with a selection from the large tubs on market stalls. For specialized foodstuffs the most fascinating place is in the old-fashioned little **Colmado Santo Domingo** in Palma on Carrer Sant Domingo, near the city tourist office. You'll spot it immediately as it's festooned with hams, sausages and strings of peppers and garlic.

MARKETS

Weekly markets are held all over the island, where everything from fresh farm produce (including live chickens) to leather bags, household linen, pots and pans, and sandals are for sale. They usually start fairly early in the morning and finish around 1pm. Particularly lively ones are held in Alcúdia on Tuesday and Sunday, in Pollença on Sunday and Sóller on Saturday. On Saturday morning in Palma, the **baratillo** (flea market) is worth a peek, even if you don't want to buy.

ENTERTAINMENT AND NIGHTLIFE

A monthly guide to events in Palma can be picked up from tourist offices. Otherwise, peruse listings in *Ultima Hora* (www.ultimahora. es/mallorca) and the *Diario de Mallorca* (www.diariodemallorca. es), both in Spanish. For English, visit the comprehensive website: www.culturalpalma.com.

Palma has a lively classical music scene. Two excellent concert halls, the Sala Magna and the Sala Mozart, are located in **Auditorium de Palma**, Passeig Marítim 18 (tel: 971 735 328 for bookings; www.auditoriumpalma.com). The Ciutat de Palma Symphony Orchestra regularly performs here, and there is a varied programme of orchestral music, ballet, jazz and opera. The **Teatre Principal**, Carrer del la Riera 2 (tel: 971 219 700; www.teatreprincipal.com) stages top-quality opera, classical recitals and jazz. In summer, concerts also take place in the music room of the **Palau March** (tel: 971 711 122; www.fundacionbmarch.es). Free outdoor performances – jazz, rock and classical – are held in the attractive setting of the **Parc de la Mar** beneath the city walls on some summer evenings. A bar serves drinks and snacks, and there's a lively party atmosphere.

LATE NIGHT LINE-UP

The bars and clubs in the big resorts thump with loud music all night long and would be hard to miss. Needless to say, they rise and fall in favour, and predicting next season's hottest spot would be unwise. They are mostly geared to the teen and early-twenties age groups, and there is no shortage of leaflets and posters trying to tempt customers.

Weekly street market in Santanyí

Summer music festival in Sant Joan

Otherwise, most of Mallorca's nightlife is to be found in Palma, where the best club is assuredly **Social** (www.wearesocial.club) on Avenida Gabriel Roca 33, a boutique nightclub with an outdoor terrace overlooking the port. Remember that the action doesn't really start until around midnight.

Outside the clubs, much of Palma's nightlife takes place in late-night bars, many of them clustered in the Sa Llotja area, where most of the restaurants can also be found. The kitsch **Abaco** (www.bar-abaco.es), on Carrer Sant Joan (off Apuntadors), with its sultry decor, caged birds, operatic background music and expensive cocktails, is an experience, as is **El Garito** (www.garitocafe.com), on Dàrsena de Can Barbarà, which has a full programme of club nights. Mallorca Rocks, also in Magaluf, hosts gigs by the coolest British bands from June to September. For all the latest information on clubbing in Magaluf, visit the website www.feelsummer.com.

CHILDREN

Sandy beaches and calm, safe waters ensure that children can remain happy on the beach for days at a time. But if that begins to pall, there are plenty of alternatives. The big resorts have a lot to offer in terms of entertainment such as waterparks; they are quite expensive, but you can easily spend a whole day in them, so you'll get your money's worth.

In S'Arenal, **Aqualand**, Palma–Arenal motorway, exit 13 (tel: 696 158 177; www.aqualand.es) with its huge water slides, claims to be the biggest aquatic park in Europe. **Western Park**, Carretera Cala Figuera–Sa Porrassa, Magaluf (tel: 626 362 859; www.westernpark.com) has adrenaline-pumping slides and high-diving exhibitions. All of the parks open daily (May–Oct) at 10am, and there are dedicated bus services from the nearby resorts.

MUSIC FESTIVALS

Summer is the time for music festivals, many held in beautiful historic buildings. The best-known one is the Deià International Music Festival (www.dimf.com). Most performances are in the stunning setting of Son Marroig. The Chopin Festival is held in the cloisters of La Cartuja in Valldemossa (www.festivalchopin.com), while the Festival de Pollença (tel: 971 899 323; www.festivalpollenca.com) attracts international musicians to the lovely cloister of Sant Domingo. There is a summer music festival with performances in Palma's Castell de Bellver and in the Jardins Fundació March in Cala Ratjada (www.fundacionbmarch.es). Sa Pobla hosts an international jazz festival in August (www.sapobla.cat), and Palma stages music events in various venues as part of the Jazz Voyeur Festival (www.jazzvoyeurfestival.es).

Coves d'Artà

In the north of the island, **Hidropark** (tel: 971 891 672; www.hidroparkalcudia.com), Avinguda Tucán, Port d'Alcúdia, caters for younger children as well so is good for all the family.

For older children and teenagers, **Magaluf Karting**, Carretera Cala Figuera–La Porrasa (tel: 971 131 734; www.kartingmagaluf.com), can be found next to the Aquapark; or **Can Picafort Karting** is located near Alcúdia (tel: 971 850 748; www.kartingcanpicafort.com).

Safari-Zoo, Ctra Porto Cristo–Cala Millor (tel: 971 810 909/10; www.safari-zoo.com), on the east coast is usually a hit. The monkeys, antelopes, elephants, giraffes and rhinos can be observed from a mini-train, or from your own car. Fascinating for adults and children is the huge **Palma Aquarium**, Carrer Manuela de los Hereros 21 (tel: 971 746 104; www.palmaaquarium.com).

Katmandu Park (tel: 971 134 660; www.katmanduparks.com) is a theme park in Magaluf mainly aimed at teens and adults, while its sister attraction in Palma Nova, Golf Fantasia (tel: 971 135 040; www.golffantasia.com), has crazy golf for all ages. Musical show Pirates Adventure (tel: 971 130 411; www.piratesadventure.com), also in Magaluf, is a spectacular evening out for all ages.

There are the Coves del Drac at Porto Cristo, the Coves d'Artà at Canyamel, and the Coves dels Hams, Carretera Porto Cristo–Manacor, which stage a digital 'virtual adventure'.

CALENDAR OF EVENTS

5–6 January: Three Kings (Reyes Magos) Procession in Palma.

16–17 January: Sant Antoni Abat festival in Palma, Artà, Sa Pobla and Manacor; a procession of animals to be blessed by their patron saint.

19–20 January: Sant Sebastià celebrated in Palma and Pollença, where the *cavallets* (small papier-mâché horses that the dancers strap round their hips) perform in a procession.

February: Carnival (Carnaval) marked in many towns and villages with fancy dress parades and general revelry. This is a pre-Lent festival, so dates vary depending on Easter.

March–April: Semana Santa (Holy Week) is commemorated in Palma and throughout the islands with solemn processions. In Pollença, the Devallament (Lowering) sees a figure of Christ brought down from the Oratori on the hill.

8–10 May: Cristianos i Moros festival, also called Ses Valentes Dones, in Sóller re-enacts a battle in 1561 when local women fought against invading Turkish pirates.

13 June: Sant Antoni de Padua festival in Artà. Lively festivities involve *cavallets* and black demons that cavort around the streets.

15–16 July: Día del Verge del Carmen, the patron saint of fishermen and sailors, is celebrated in many ports with processions on the water. Palma, Port de Sóller and Cala Ratjada are the principal venues.

Late July: Sant Jaume in Alcúdia is a big religious and secular festival.

24 August: Sant Bartomeu is celebrated in Capdepera and Montuïri with horse races and devil dancers.

28 August: Sant Agustí fiesta in Felanitx, with *cavallets* (carousels) and *cabezudos* (big papier-mache heads).

First Sunday in September: Processó de la Beatá in Santa Margalida.

Last Sunday in September or first in October: the Festa dies Butifarró in Sant Joan, with folk dancing and feasting on the famous Mallorcan black pudding *(butifarró)*.

31 December: Festa de Standa in Palma commemorating the Christian reconquest of the island under Jaume I in 1229, with a procession.

FOOD AND DRINK

Restaurants in Mallorca cover a wide spectrum, from the excellent to the mediocre, from the local to the international. You will find traditional, rural cooking – the hearty *cuina mallorquina* – as well as ubiquitous Spanish dishes like *paella* and *gazpacho* that are very popular, though they have little to do with the island. There has also been a recent emphasis on Basque cooking, regarded as one of the best regional cuisines in Spain. You will also find refined dishes infused with a French flair in the more expensive restaurants. A clutch of top-notch chefs are working on the island and, while a meal in one of their restaurants is not cheap, it is considerably less expensive than it would be in one of the European

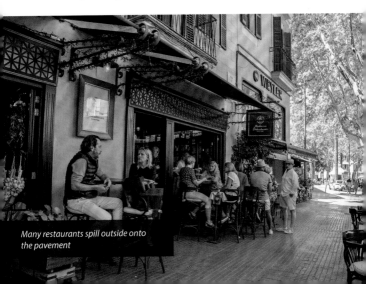

Many restaurants spill outside onto the pavement

capitals. At the other end of the market, there are, of course, such staples as chicken and chips, pizza, bratwurst and sauerkraut for people staying in the popular resort towns and prefer to stick with what they know.

CUINA MALLORQUINA

Much of the best cooking derives from simple, country fare, cooked in olive oil and made from whatever fresh ingredients are in season. *Cuina mallorquina* reaches its height in *cellers* (see page 72) but can be found in many other places, too. A meal usually starts with a dish of multicoloured, oddly shaped and quite delicious olives and a basket of rough-textured bread being brought to the table. There is sometimes a small charge for this, though often it is on the house.

Sopas mallorquinas – invariably referred to in this plural form – is a combination of vegetables, olives, garlic and sometimes pork. It is more like stew than soup, and makes a substantial first course. The *sopas* is usually served in an earthenware bowl, or *greixera de terra*, which in turn gives its name to a complete range of casseroles: *greixonera de peix* is a fish stew, and *greixonera d'alberginies* or *berenjenas* in Castilian is a wonderful aubergine concoction.

Another speciality is *tumbet*, a dish of peppers, aubergines, tomatoes and potatoes, coated in beaten egg and baked in the oven. This usually features as a first course, but can be very filling, so should be followed by something fairly light. *Frit mallorquí* is a tasty mixture of strips of fried liver and kidney, peppers and leeks.

MEAT

Every rural family on the island once kept pigs, and many still do. Pork and its by-products are a mainstay, with local specialities including *butifarró* (a spicy sausage, either white or dark); *sobrasada*, a bright red, pork-and-red-pepper sausage with a consistency

Caldereta de langosta, or lobster casserole

rather like pâté; and *jamón serrano* or *jamón iberico*, a delicious cured ham, cut from a whole piece hanging from the ceiling.

Other popular dishes are *llomb amb col* (pork with cabbage and raisins); and *arròs brut* (rice with pork or chicken). *Lechona asada* (roast suckling pig) is traditionally a Christmas dish but may sometimes be found on menus at other times.

You don't see a great many cows in Mallorca, so there's not a lot of beef in the restaurants, though some of the more expensive places serve delicious steaks. Chicken – *pollo* – is fairly common, while goat – *cabrito* – turns up on country menus, usually grilled, sometimes in a stew. Rabbit *(conejo)*, is popular, sometimes served in a *greixonera* (stew), or *à la plancha* – grilled, and accompanied by *allioli*, a garlic mayonnaise; *conejo con caracoles* – rabbit with snails – is a local favourite.

Snails (*caracoles*) are something of an acquired taste, but one that the islanders acquired long ago. At times, they can be a free source of protein: after it has rained, you'll see people out carrying string bags full of sand. They're searching for snails, which they clean by leaving them for several days in the sand, before cooking them and then eating them with *allioli*. Purists insist that true *allioli*, which is sometimes also served with the bread and olives that arrive at the start of a meal, should be made simply with oil and garlic, without the addition of eggs.

FISH

Really fresh fish and seafood are becoming something of a luxury on Mallorca. The seas have been over-fished and local fishermen, in any case, could not keep up with demand in summer. If you ask, waiters will usually tell you honestly that much of the fish they serve is imported, frozen, from Spain's Atlantic ports. *Salmonete* (red mullet) is caught locally, so are sardines *(sardinas)* and some of the *langostas*, spiny lobsters that are found on many menus. Locally caught *cap roig* – scorpion fish – is the choice Mallorcan fish; the cheeks are considered a great delicacy. *Caldereta de langosta* (*llagosta* in Mallorquí), a delicious lobster casserole, is a Menorquin dish, and an expensive one, that appears on some Mallorcan menus. *Zarzuela de mariscos* can be excellent – a thick stew of shellfish, tomatoes, garlic, wine and almonds.

BREAKING BREAD (AND POURING OIL)

Mallorca, whose landscape is dotted with ancient, gnarled olive trees and once-functional windmills, is renowned for its bread and oil – so much so that Tomás Graves, the son of Robert, wrote an entire book about it, *Bread & Oil: Majorcan Culture's Last Stand*. The bread is dense and biscuit coloured, the oil thick and rich and green. So it is not surprising that *pa amb oli*, bread and oil (pronounced *pamboli*), is served everywhere. It is simply toasted bread rubbed with garlic, sprinkled with salt and drizzled with olive oil. As a refinement, it may also be flavoured with fresh tomatoes (*pa amb tomàquet*) and served with cheese, local ham, *sobrasada* or tuna. Cafés called *pambolierias* will give you your chosen ingredients on a large platter, plus a bottle of olive oil, and leave you to make yourself a tasty, filling and budget-friendly snack.

Farmed trout (*trucha*), sole (*lenguado*) and hake (*merluza*), which are mostly imported into the islands frozen, also feature on many a menu. Squid (*calamares*), cuttlefish (*sepia*) and octopus (*pulpo*), cooked in a variety of ways, are also widely available. *Calamares en su tinta* is squid cooked in its own ink; *a la romana* means it is cut into rings and fried in batter – excellent when fresh and not over-battered. *Bacalao* is cod, salted and dried, and not to everyone's taste, but when well prepared, it can be good, especially in *esqueixada*, a salad of tomatoes, onions, beans and shredded salt cod.

SWEETS AND PUDDINGS

Home-made *crema catalana*, or its mass-produced cousin, known as *flan*, is as ubiquitous in the Balearics as the mainland, but there are also some tempting sweet pastries and the almond and honey desserts that are a legacy of the Moorish occupation. Fig cake, a rich, dark brown confection with the consistency of Christmas pudding, is particularly popular in and around Sóller, a town also known for its *picos de mazapán* – little white pyramids of marzipan. Vegetarians should be aware that lard (*saim*) is an essential Mallorcan ingredient. It is a key element in the *ensaïmada*, a light, airy pastry that's rolled up like a turban, dusted with sugar, and eaten for breakfast, sometimes dipped in coffee.

Binissalem produces a good range of wines

DRINKS

Wine is usually drunk with meals, much of it imported from the Spanish mainland; Riojas and varieties from the Catalan Penedès region feature prominently. But island wines are good, too, and some restaurants (especially the *cellers*) specialize in them.

> ### Fruit for dessert
>
> There is also fruit, of course: sweet melons, juicy oranges, peaches and nectarines, fresh figs and grapes, all the better because they are locally grown and have ripened in the field, not in transit.

Most come from the region around Binissalem, which lies between Palma and Inca. Spanish beer is also quite popular. Fresh orange juice *(zumo de naranja)* is refreshing and delicious; and those who like the flavour of almonds should try *horchata de chufa*, a milky drink made from ground almonds and served ice-cold in summer. A local aperitif is *palo*, made from carobs and herbs and produced in Bunyola; and angel d'or, made in Sóller, is a local orange liqueur.

EATING HABITS

Local people eat late; lunch is between 1.30pm and 4pm, and any time before 9.30pm or 10pm is regarded early for dinner. However, restaurateurs, aware that northern European visitors like to eat earlier, have adapted their timetables accordingly. Remember that a restaurant that may look empty and unloved at 8pm might be packed and popular by 10pm. As breakfast is insubstantial – coffee and toast or a croissant – lunch is often the main meal. Islanders generally have three courses, but it's perfectly acceptable to share a first course, or to order *un sólo plato* – just a main course.

Many restaurants offer a *menú del día*, a daily set menu that is a real bargain; this is always available at lunchtime, and occasionally in the evening as well. For a fixed price, you get three courses – a starter, often soup or salad, a main dish and dessert, which is usually

Tapas is a staple in Mallorca

ice cream, a piece of fruit or a *flan*, plus bread, and a glass of wine, beer or bottled water. In restaurants where local people are eating, you will notice that many of them order the *menú*, an indication that it is not one specially designed for tourists.

Reservations are necessary only at the more expensive restaurants or places that are popular for Sunday lunch. Prices may or may not include VAT (IVA). Bills sometimes include service – look out for *servicio incluido*. If not, it is customary to leave a 10 percent tip.

TAPAS

Tapas, the small plates that have become popular far beyond the borders of Spain, form a major part of eating out in Mallorca – at least in the larger towns. They are still eaten as snacks, with drinks, which was their original role, but it is now common for a selection of tapas, or *raciones*, which are larger portions, to take the place of a main meal, which can be a relatively inexpensive way to eat. The size of portions varies between restaurants, so be guided by a waiter as to how many dishes to order. Favourites include stuffed squid (*calamares rellenos*), *pimientos de padrón* (small, green peppers grilled whole and sprinkled with sea salt), *chorizo*, and *espinacas à la catalana* (spinach cooked with garlic, anchovies, raisins and pine nuts). All are served with fresh bread to mop up the sauces and complement the strong flavours.

BARS AND CAFÉS

Bars and cafés are an important institution in Spanish life. In towns, some open at first light to cater for early-morning workers and most are open by 8.30am for breakfast. One of the great pleasures of the Mediterranean is sitting in a square in the morning with a *café con leche* and *ensaïmada* and watching a town come to life. In resorts, however, where many bars are open late at night and many tourists breakfast in their hotels, you may struggle to find somewhere for an early coffee.

Wines and spirits are served at all hours. It is usually around 10 percent cheaper to have a drink at the bar than at a table. Sitting on a stool at the bar can make you feel like one of the locals, too, though relaxing at an outside table and watching the world go by is another simple pleasure.

Can Joan de S'Aigo in Palma, artist Joan Miró's favourite café

TO HELP YOU ORDER

Could we have a table? **¿Nos puede dar una mesa, por favor?**
Do you have a set menu? **¿Tiene un menú del día?**
I would like... **Quisiera…**
The bill, please **La cuenta, por favor**

DECIPHERING THE MENU

agua water
vino wine
leche milk
cerveza beer
pan bread
entremeses hors-d'oeuvre
ensalada salad
tortilla omelette
pescado fish
mariscos shellfish
langosta lobster
calamares squid
mejillones mussels
anchoas anchovies
atún tuna
bacalao dried cod
cangrejo crab
pulpitos baby octopus
trucha trout
carne meat
cerdo/lomo pork
ternera veal
cordero lamb
buey/res beef
pollo chicken

conejo rabbit
poco hecho rare
al punto medium
buen hecho well done
asado roast
a la plancha grilled
al ajillo in garlic
picante spicy
salsa sauce
cocido stew
jamón Serrano cured ham
chorizo spicy sausage
morcilla black pudding
bocadillo sandwich
arroz rice
verduras vegetables
champiñones mushrooms
judías beans
espinacas spinach
cebollas onions
lentejas lentils
queso cheese
postre dessert
helado ice cream
azúcar sugar

WHERE TO EAT

Each restaurant and café reviewed in this Guide is accompanied by a price category, based on the cost of a three-course meal (or similar) for one, including a glass of house wine:

€€€€ **over 80 euros**
€€€ **60–80 euros**
€€ **40–60 euros**
€ **below 40 euros**

PALMA

13% € *Carrer Sant Feliu 13a, tel: 971 425 187;* www.13porciento.com. Just off Passeig des Born, this attractive wine bar serves excellent plates of local charcuterie as well as fish and meat courses, paired with an excellent selection of wine. Mon–Sat 12.30–11.30pm & Sun 6–11.30pm.

Bar Bosch € *Plaça Rei Joan Carles I 6, tel: 971 71 22 28.* One of the most popular and inexpensive tapas bars in town, with a modest interior and a heaving pavement terrace. The traditional haunt of the city's intellectuals, and usually humming with conversation. Sun–Thurs 8am–11pm, Fri & Sat until midnight.

Bon Lloc € *Carrer Sant Feliu 7, tel: 971 718 617;* www.bonllocrestaurant.com. Palma's oldest and best vegetarian restaurant is situated on the ground floor of a sixteenth-century palace in the old town. The menu changes daily, and its mouthwatering dishes mean the place is popular with carnivores too. Mon–Sat 1–4pm, Thurs–Sat also 8–11pm.

Café Gran € *Hotel Plaça Weyler 3, tel: 971 72 80 77.* Set on the ground floor of the eponymous hotel, a handsome *Moderniste* building of 1903, this trim, modern café makes a good spot for coffee and a light bite, with tables inside or out on a pleasant little square. Daily 8am–10pm.

Ca'n Eduardo €€€ *Carrer Contramoll Mollet s/n, tel: 971 721 182;* www.caneduardo.com. Occupying the top floor of an unassuming, three-floor block beside the city's fishing harbour, this excellent restaurant surprises with a superb range of fish dishes. Laidback but buzzy atmosphere. Daily 1–11pm.

Celler Pagès €€ *Carrer Felip Bauza 2, off Carrer Estanc, tel: 971 726 036;* www.cellerpages.com. Small and intimate restaurant with a family atmosphere serving traditional Mallorcan food – try the tongue with capers. Reservations advised. Wed–Sat 1–3.30pm & 8–11pm.

Celler Sa Premsa € *Plaça Bisbe Berenguer de Palou 8, tel: 971 723 529;* www.cellersapremsa.com. A local institution, with over sixty years under its belt. It pairs great ambience with a wide selection of classic, filling Mallorcan dishes. Mon–Sat noon–4pm & 7.30pm–11pm.

Forn de Sant Joan €€ *Carrer Sant Joan 4, tel: 971 728 422;* www.forndesant-joan.com. Dining rooms spread across multiple floors, in the heart of the old town restaurant area. A la carte Mediterranean dishes available, but it's essentially upmarket tapas – and very nice too. Daily 1–4pm & 6.30–11pm.

La Bodeguilla €€ *Carrer Sant Jaume 3,* www.la-bodeguilla.com. Slick and smooth establishment with subtle lighting in the heart of the city, just off Plaça Rei Joan Carles I. The premises are divided into two – a small tapas and wine bar and a slightly larger restaurant, though tapas is served here too. It's the tapas you want, an exquisite range of Spanish/Catalan dishes – try, for example, the oxtail in a red wine sauce or the razor shell with pickled, roasted tomatoes. Sun–Thurs 1–10.30pm, Fri & Sat until 11pm.

Marc Fosh €€€ *Carrer de la Missió, 7A, tel: 971 720 114;* www.marcfosh.com. Epicurean dining at a Michelin-starred restaurant. An experimental menu drawing on local produce from across the Balearic Islands, served in an enjoyable ambience. Also offers wine tasting for oenophiles. Advance booking essential. Tues–Sat 1.30pm–3pm & 7.30pm–9.30pm.

Safrà 21 €€ *Carrer Illa de Corfú 21, Ciudad Jardin, tel: 971 263 670;* www.safra21.com. At lunchtime, this restaurant specializes in serving traditional rice dishes whereas, come evening, it morphs into Mallorca's first 'bistronomic' restaurant, focusing on top-quality cuisine at reasonable prices. Out near the airport. Daily 1–3.30pm, plus Fri & Sat 8–10.30pm.

Trattoria Sant Ambros € *Plaça Coll 11*, www.st-ambros.com. There's the Sant Ambros café on one side of this little square, the trattoria on the other. The trattoria menu covers all the Italian classics, and although the food isn't fantastic, it is inexpensive and the portions are substantial. Plaça Coll, on the edge of the Sa Gerrería neighbourhood, is a great place to savour the city. Daily 8am–10pm.

THE WESTERN CORNER
Andratx

Sa Societat De Ca Na Fornera €€ *Av. Juan Carlos I, 19, tel: 971 236 566*. Authentic Spanish cuisine at its best. Hospitable ambience, traditional meals and local wine. Sun & Mon 8am–4pm, Wed–Sat 8am–4pm & 7–10.30pm.

Banyalbufar

Son Tomás €€ *Carrer Baronia 17, tel: 971 618 149*. A small and cosy bar-restaurant whose outdoor dining terrace commands outstanding views of the beautiful coast. Fish comes directly from the boats in the cove; *paella* and the *arroz negro* (black rice) are highly recommended. Wed–Mon 12.30–3.30pm & 7.30–9.30pm.

THE WEST COAST
Deià

El Barrigon Xelini € *Archiduc Lluis Salvador 19, tel: 971 639 139*. Loud and lively, this popular place on the main village road specializes in tapas, and they come in all varieties. The stuffed squid is extremely good; the staff are friendly and casual; there's an outside terrace open in the summer months. Tues–Sun 12.30pm–10pm.

Es Racó d'es Teix €€€€ *Carrer Sa Vinya Veia 6, tel: 971 639 501;* http://esracodesteix.es. Chef Josef Saueschell is the man behind the menu at Es Racó d'es Teix, rustling together contemporary cuisine in satisfying portions; he's won a Michelin star for his efforts. The *ballontine conejo* (medallions of rabbit) is delicious. Wed–Sun 1–3pm & 7.30–10pm.

Sebastian €€€€ *Carrer Felipe Bauza 2, tel: 971 639 417;* www.restaurantese-bastian.com. Lobster with asparagus ravioli and fig fritter with white chocolate mousse are just two reasons to eat at this rustic-but-stylish restaurant, where the Mediterranean cuisine often has a touch of the Far East. Open daily for dinner only; closed Wed.

Sóller

Bens d'Avall €€€ *Urb Costa Deià, Carretera Sóller-Deià, km56 tel: 971 632 381;* www.bensdavall.com. Situated about half-way between Sóller and Deià, this gourmet restaurant with a lovely outdoor dining terrace overlooking the sea specializes in New Balearic Cuisine made with local produce. Wed–Sun 1–3pm.

Sa Cova €€ *Plaça Constitució 7, Sóller, tel: 971 633 222.* Pleasant restaurant on the main square. Serves good *conejo* (rabbit), which is popular in the area. The seafood stew – *cazuela* – is worth the trip too. Daily noon–10pm.

THE NORTH
Alcúdia

Basico Steak House €€ *Carrer Serra 22, tel: 871 047 849.* Prettily located in the narrow streets of the old town, this popular restaurant, with its dinky courtyard and elongated windows, is the place to go for steaks; barbecued steaks, to be exact. Daily except Wed 1–10pm.

Cala Sant Vicenç

Lavanda €€€ *Carrer Maressers 2, tel: 971 530 250;* www.hotelcala.com. An excellent restaurant situated in the *Cala Sant Vicenç* hotel (see page 138). The menu features refined Mediterranean cooking, and there's an excellent wine list to wash it all down with. Set menu available. Open daily for dinner; closed Dec–Jan.

Pollença

Bar Nou Restaurante €€ *Carrer d'Antoni Maura, 13, Pollença, tel: 971 530 005;* www.barnourestaurante.com. Established in 1997, this cosy restaurant is run by the Torres family, and is known for its *paella* and tasty tapas. You can expect delicious meals with flavours of home-made food. Daily except Tues 12.30–3pm & 7–10pm.

Celler Es Molí €€ *Carrer Pare Vives 72, tel: 971 531 950.* Well off the beaten track, in an ancient building on the corner of a narrow side street, this welcoming restaurant offers authentic Mallorcan/Spanish cuisine at very affordable prices. The fish soup is especially tasty. Fri–Tues 1.30–3.30pm & 7–10pm, Wed 1.30–3.30pm.

Port de Pollença

Bellaverde Vegan & Vegetarian Restaurant € *Carrer de les Monges 14, tel: 675 602 528.* The only specialist vegetarian restaurant in this part of the island. Here, you can enjoy your food in the shadow of century-year-old fig trees. Tues–Sun 8.30am–11.30pm.

Stay €€ *Moll Nou s/n, tel: 971 864 013;* www.stayrestaurant.com. A stylish restaurant situated right by the water in the centre of the port, the fittingly named *Stay* has been around for years. Fish is the first choice but there are meat dishes on the menu too, including lamb and pigeon ravioli. Open every day of the year. Daily 9am–10.30pm.

THE CENTRAL PLAIN
Inca

Joan Marc €€ *Plaça del Blanquer 10, tel: 971 500 804;* www.joanmarcrestaurant.com. The locals' choice for the best restaurant in town, the excellent *Joan Marc* offers a chic but affordable take on classic Mallorquín dishes. Tues–Sun 7–10pm, plus Thurs–Sat 1–3.30pm.

Petra

Es Celler €€ *Carrer de l'Hospital 46, tel: 971 561 056;* www.restaurantesceller. com. Huge and cavernous restaurant serving up heaped plates of traditional food, including meat roasted in a wood oven. Tues–Sun noon–11pm.

Sineu

Celler de Ca'n Font €€ *Sa Plaça, Sineu, tel: 971 520 313;* www.canfontsineu.com. This traditional *celler*, situated in a hotel of the same name (see page 141), is the place to go for excellent *sopas mallorquinas*, roast suckling pig and classic rice dishes. Mon–Sat 7–11pm, plus Wed 9am–3.30pm & Fri–Sun 1–3.30pm.

THE EAST AND SOUTHEAST
Artà

Finca Es Serral € *Cami Cala Torta, tel: 971 835 336;* http://fincaesserral.com. Enjoy Mallorcan and vegetarian cuisine in the rustic dining room or on the outdoor terrace of this attractive farm on the outskirts of town. Daily except Mon noon–4pm & 7–11pm. Closed Nov–March.

Cala Figuera

Es Port € *Carrer Virgen del Carmen 88, tel: 971 165 140.* Eat inside or out, overlooking the bay. Spanish and Mallorcan specialities, fresh fish and signature pizzas. Daily except Tues 12.30pm–10.30pm.

Cala Millor

Tapas de Sa Caleta €€ *Passeig Marítim, 3, tel: 971 58 68 34;* http://sacaleta-calamillor.com. Great service and even better food. As the name suggests, tapas is the specialty here. However, the menu is varied enough to cater to all tastes. Daily 8am–11.30pm.

Porto Cristo

Vibes by Quince €€ Carrer Bordils 51, *tel: 971 820 796;* www.restaurante-vibes.com. You may be tempted to eat here just for the view, as the restaurant is situated right on the water. However, *Vibes by Quince*'s popularity is as much about its excellent fresh fish dishes as it is the sublime vistas. Daily 11am–10.30pm.

TRAVEL ESSENTIALS

PRACTICAL INFORMATION

A

ACCESSIBLE TRAVEL

Palma airport and most modern hotels have wheelchair access and facilities for travellers with disabilities. There are also wheelchair-friendly buses. On the other hand, suitable public toilet facilities are a rarity, few taxis are disability-friendly, and car-rental companies are, generally speaking, poorly stocked with adapted vehicles.

ACCOMMODATION (See also Camping, and the list of Recommended Hotels on page 133)

Almost everywhere, hotel prices are governed by the season, with peak months (around June to August) costing much more than the shoulder and off-seasons; note, however, that many hotels in the resort areas close between November and March. In season, the majority of large resort hotels are block-booked by package tour operators. Breakfast is often, but not always, included in a room rate; check before booking. A value-added tax (IVA) of 10 percent and the sustainable tourism tax ("tourist tax"; €4, €3, €2 or €1 per night, depending on the type of accommodation; under 16s go free) are added to the total; the tourist tax is halved on the ninth day.

Accommodation ranges across a broad spectrum, although there are few pensions (guest houses). *Hostales* (modest hotels) are graded from one to three stars while *hoteles* (hotels) are rated from one to five stars. In recent years, there has been an ever-growing wave of boutique hotels on the scene, along with luxury resorts. Grades are more a reflection of facilities than quality: some two-star places can be superior to others with four. A new category – the *hotel d'interior* – has been introduced. These are small hotels (no more than eight rooms) that must be in traditional buildings, however minimalist their interior decoration may be.

Small hotels in rural settings and refurbished farmhouses and manor houses are called *finca* or *agroturisme* properties. They range from rustic to luxurious, and many have minimum four- or seven-day stays. Rural Hotels Mallorca (www.ruralhotelsmallorca.com) has a particularly good range, albeit at the boutique end of the market.

All-in package deals can often be the cheapest option for visitors to Mallorca and provide a budget-friendly base for exploring the island. If you want to rent a villa or apartment, there are numerous agencies: www.majorcanvillas.com and www.mallorca.co.uk are reliable ones. Finally, there is the opportunity to stay in a hilltop monastery or sanctuary, of which there are about eight (check the Where to Go section for details). The most accessible is the *Monestir de Lluc* (www.lluc.net). The tourist office near the cathedral in Palma (see page 130) can provide a full list. These are fairly austere, but extremely economical and popular with local people and outdoor enthusiasts.

I would like a single/double room **Quisiera una habitación sencilla/doble**
With/without bathroom and toilet/shower **con/sin baño/ducha**
What's the rate per night? **¿Cuál es el precio por noche?**
Is breakfast included? **¿Está incluído el desayuno?**

AIRPORT

Palma de Mallorca International Airport (PMI) is a sprawling affair located about 12km (7.5 miles) east of the city centre (www.palmaairport.info). Taxis and buses link the airport with Palma; bus No. 1 leaves the airport every 15 minutes from 6am to 1.10am (until 2am in summer), running to Plaça d'Espanya and on to the port, with stops en route (fare €5); the journey time to Plaça d'Espanya is around 30 minutes. There is a bus stop in front of the Arrivals Hall. Taxi is a little faster than the bus, taking around 15–20 minutes, traffic permitting. They line up outside Arrivals; the approximate fare is €25.

B

BICYCLE AND SCOOTER HIRE

A practical and enjoyable way to see the island is by bike, and you'll find rental outfits in most resorts – hotels and tourist offices have leaflets, and you'll be handed flyers in the street. Note, however, that you need to be very fit to tackle the steep roads of the Serra de Tramuntana mountains; cyclists are not allowed to use the island's main tunnel on the road between Palma and Sóller. Mopeds and scooters are also available, but you will need a special licence. Prices vary widely, so shop around. Remember that a helmet is compulsory when riding a motorcycle, whatever the engine size. Ask for a helmet and for a pump and puncture kit, in case you get stuck with a flat tire miles from your hotel, and always carry ID. In Palma, try Palma by Bike, Avinguda Antoni Maura 10 (tel: 971 718 062, www.palmaonbike.com). Pro Cycle Hire, in Port de Pollença, will deliver your bike direct to your resort hotel if arranged in advance (tel: 971 866 857, www.procyclehire.com)

BUDGETING FOR YOUR TRIP

Mallorca once had a reputation for being cheap and cheerful, but while it's still possible to have an inexpensive holiday here – think monastery accommodation, for example – the island as a whole has moved upmarket. All prices below are approximate and given only as a guide.

Getting there. Air fares vary enormously. Flights from the UK with a budget airline can range from around £90 return off-season to £250 or more in high season. See www.skyscanner.net to compare prices.

Accommodation. Hotels can be more expensive than on the Spanish mainland (for approximate prices in Recommended Hotels, see page 133). Rates for two sharing a double room during high season can start at €85 in a *hostal* to €400 at a top-of-the-range hotel. A comfortable, pleasant three-star hotel will cost about €100–150. Rates drop considerably out of season.

Meals. The *menú del día*, a fixed-price midday meal, is usually an excellent bargain, costing around €20 for a decent three-course meal, including one drink included. In a bar, a continental breakfast (fresh orange juice, coffee, croissant) costs around €8; a coffee €3–€8. The average price of a three-course a la carte meal, including house wine, will nudge €40 per person. You can pay considerably less, but at top restaurants, expect to pay up to double that figure. The price of wine has risen; a glass of wine in a smartish bar will set you back around €7.

Attractions. Most museums and galleries charge an entry fee of €3–5. Entry to La Real Cartuja, Valldemossa, costs €12; the Coves del Drach around €16. Waterparks are more expensive, creeping up to €25 (children €18). A two-hour trip in a glass-bottomed boat costs around €20 (children half-price). You can usually find discounted and advance tickets online.

Ferries. Interisland ferries between Mallorca and Menorca are reasonable for foot passengers (about €50 return), but are more expensive if you take a car (between €100 and €300 for a vehicle and two passengers). The ferry from Mallorca to Ibiza is around the same price. Deals are often available, especially if you book well in advance. Note, however, that car rental companies do not allow their vehicles to be taken from one Balearic island to another.

CAR HIRE

Public transport is excellent, but if you do want to travel to every corner of the island, hiring a car is advisable. Major international companies – Avis, Hertz, Budget, Europcar – and Spanish national companies have offices at the airport and in Palma as well as in the major resorts. Many have weekly specials, which can work out as little as €30–40 per day. Rates are seasonal, and usually lower if booked online well in advance. Third-party insurance is included, but comprehensive insurance – *todo riesgo* – is usually extra. Be aware that insurance may not cover you for off-road driving, and in-car satnavs often incur a hefty charge. In addition to value-added tax (IVA) of 21 percent, an extra eco-tax of €3–7 a day is payable – the exact rate depends on the vehicle.

Drivers must be at least 18 or 21 (minimum age varies depending on car type) and have (generally) held a licence for at least six months. Hire companies will accept your national driver's licence.

Avis: Mallorca airport, tel: 902 110 261; www.avis.es

Europcar: Mallorca airport, tel: 911 505 000; www.europcar.com
Gold Car: Mallorca airport, tel: 918 341 400; www.goldcar.es
Hertz: Mallorca airport, tel: 971 789 670; www.hertz.es
Hiper: Mallorca airport, tel: 971 269 911; www.hiperrentacar.com

I'd like to rent a car. **Quisiera alquilar un coche.**
for one day/week. **por un día/una semana.**
Please include full insurance. **Haga el favor de incluir el seguro a todo riesgo.**

CLIMATE

The sea is balmy for swimming from June to October. July and August can be scorching, and humidity may be high. Spring and autumn lure walkers and birdwatchers and those who enjoy sightseeing in cooler temperatures. Mallorca enjoys a mild winter, and many hotels stay open during the winter months. It can be chilly and wet at times, but a wall of mountains along the northwest coast protects the rest of the island from the worst of the weather.

The average temperatures below apply to Palma, but do not vary greatly throughout the islands, except in the mountainous areas.

	J	F	M	A	M	J	J	A	S	O	N	D
°C	10	11	12	14	17	22	24	24	22	18	14	12
°F	50	51	54	58	63	71	76	76	72	65	57	53

CLOTHING

In summer, you only need lightweight cotton clothes – though in June and September, you may need a jacket or jumper for the evening. Remember, also, to pack a sunhat and something with sleeves to cover your shoulders. During the rest of the year, a light jacket and an umbrella will come in handy.

Although the tendency is towards casual dress, some restaurants, bars and clubs object to men wearing shorts and T-shirts and women being too 'skimpily' dressed.

Walking shoes or good-quality trainers are essential if you are planning any long treks.

CRIME AND SAFETY (See also Emergencies)

Spain's crime rate has caught up with that of other European countries, and the Balearics is not immune, though they remain one of the safest places in Europe. Be on your guard against purse-snatchers and pickpockets near Palma Cathedral and around the Plaça Major at night, and in markets and other crowded places. Take the same precautions as you would at home. In Palma, report thefts and break-ins to the Policía Nacional; elsewhere, to the Guardia Civil. You need a police report for insurance purposes.

I want to report a theft. **Quiero denunciar un robo.**

D

DRIVING

Road conditions. There is a stretch of motorway around Palma and its bay, west towards Andratx, ending at Peguera, and east to Llucmajor. Another motorway runs north from Palma, via Inca, and continues behind the town to Alcúdia. If you're driving from Sóller towards Palma, a tunnel carved through the mountains cuts driving time. There's a good straight road running east–west across the island. Secondary roads are narrow but generally good; on the mountainous northwest coast a series of hairpin bends tests the mettle of anxious drivers. Some of the mountain roads are nerve-jangling and are best avoided after rain.

Rules and regulations. Drive on the right, overtake on the left, yield to vehicles coming from the right. Seat belts are compulsory. Children under 12 must travel in the rear. Speed limits are 120km/h (75mph) on motorways, 100km/h (60mph) on two-lane highways, 90km/h (56mph) on other main roads, 50km/h (32mph), or as marked, in densely populated areas.

Traffic police. Roads are patrolled (strictly) by the Guardia Civil de Tráfico, on motorcycles. Fines are payable on the spot. The permitted blood-alcohol level is low, and penalties are stiff.

Fuel. Service stations are plentiful. Petrol *(gasolina)* comes in 90 (super lead-free) and 98 (lead-free super plus) grades. Diesel fuel is widely available, too. Electric car-charging points are increasing at a rate of knots.

Parking. Underground carparks have made life much easier for drivers in Palma (the one in Av. Antoni Maura by the cathedral as you enter town is a good one), while parking is less of a problem elsewhere. Most towns have metered areas, denoted by a 'P' and blue lines on the road.

Mechanical problems. Garages are efficient, but repairs may take time in busy areas. For emergencies, call the 112. If you have broken down, call the emergency number provided by your car-hire company or, if it is your own vehicle, your car insurance company,

Road signs. Most are standard pictographs; the phrases below may also be useful.

Aparcamiento Parking
Desviación Detour
Obras Road works
Peatones Pedestrians
Peligro Danger
Salida de camiones Truck exit
Senso único One way
Useful expressions:
¿Se puede aparcar aquí? Can I park here?
Ha habido un accidente. There has been an accident.

E

ELECTRICITY

Spanish electricity runs at 220 volts AC, with standard European-style, two-pin plugs. Brits will need a plug adaptor to connect their appliances; North Americans should bring both an adaptor and a transformer in order to connect their electrical appliances.

EMBASSIES AND CONSULATES

The following are consulates:

UK: Carrer Convent dels Caputxins 4, Palma, tel: 933 666 200;
www.gov.uk
US: Carrer Porto Pi 8, Palma, tel: 971 403 707;
https://es.usembassy.gov.
Ireland: Carrer Sant Miquel 68, Palma, tel: 971 719 244;
https://www.dfa.ie/irish-embassy/Spain.

Australia, Canada, New Zealand and South Africa have no consulates located on the island of Mallorca; their nearest embassies are situated in Madrid.

> Where is the British/American consulate? **¿Dónde está el consulado británico/americano?**

EMERGENCIES

General emergency number (police, fire, ambulance): 112
National Police: 091
Municipal Police: 092
Guardia Civil (traffic): 062
Ambulance: 061
Fire: 080

Police! **Policía!**
Help! **Socorro!**
Fire! **Fuego!**
Stop! **Deténgase!**
Go away! **Váyase!**

G

GETTING THERE

Air travel (see also Airports). Palma de Mallorca's airport is connected with London and most other UK cities by regular non-stop flights, as well as frequent flights from many other European cities.

For information on flights from the UK, check out the websites of Iberia (www.iberia.com) and British Airways (www.britishairways.com). From Eire, it's Aer Lingus (www.aerlingus.com). Numerous budget airlines, including easyJet (www.easyJet.com), Flybe (www.flybe.com), Jet 2 (www.jet2.com), Ryanair (www.ryanair.com) and Vueling (www.vueling.com), fly to Palma from airports all over the UK. Excellent bargains can be found for those willing to travel at very short notice, both for flight-only tickets and for packages that include accommodation.

By sea. Car ferries run daily from Barcelona and Valencia to Palma. The slower, overnight trip takes eight hours to Palma on Trasmediterránea (Moll de Paraires, Estació Marítima 2, Palma, www.trasmediterranea.es). Baleària has services from Barcelona to Palma (7.5 hours) and to Port d'Alcúdia, which takes 6.5 hours (Moll de Paraires 3, Estació Marítima, Palma, www.balearia.com). It also provides a daily service from Dénia to Palma, which takes around 5.5 hours.

GUIDES AND TOURS

Local tourist offices may have details of guided tours in the area, but here is a selection of the more interesting ones:

Mallorca Hiking: tel: 699 906 009; www.mallorcahiking.com. A wide range of guided walks with different themes – strenuous hikes, gastronomy, architecture – for all levels.

Mallorcan Walking Tours (MWT): www.mallorcanwalkingtours.com. MWT's excellent programme of guided treks covers the whole of the Serra de Tramuntana, as well as the hilly uplands north of Sant Elm.

Mallorca Wine Tours: tel: 653 528 659; www.mallorcawinetours.com. Tours of Mallorca's vineyards on a small tourist train.

Palma City Sightseeing: tel: 902 101 081; www.city-sightseeing-spain.com/en/home. Open-top bus tours of Palma.

Tramuntana Tours: tel: 971 632 423; www.tramuntanatours.com. Walking, mountain biking and sea-kayaking in small groups.

H

HEALTH AND MEDICAL CARE

Standards of hygiene are generally high; the most common problems visitors encounter will be due to an excess of sun or alcohol. Tap water is perfectly safe, though many visitors stick resolutely to the bottled stuff. *Agua con gas* is carbonated, *agua sin gas* is still.

First-aid personnel *(practicantes)* make daily rounds of the larger resort hotels; some hotels have a nurse on duty. Many resorts have medical centres *(centros medicos)*, privately run institutions with English-speaking staff, where health-care services must be paid for on the spot, in cash or by credit card.

Under reciprocal health-care arrangements, all citizens of the EU (European Union) and EEA (European Economic Area) are entitled to free medical treatment within Spain's public health-care system. The UK is, of course, no longer part of the EU, but its citizens are still entitled to free, albeit limited, access to Spain's public health-care system if they are in possession of a GHIC (Global Health Insurance Card), which is itself a replacement for the European Health Insurance Card (EHIC). Other non-EU/EEA nationals are not generally entitled to free treatment and should, therefore, take out their own medical insurance. That said, EU/EEA/UK citizens may want to consider private health insurance too, to cover the cost of items not within the EU/EEA/UK schemes, such as dental treatment and repatriation on medical grounds. No inoculations are currently required for Mallorca or Menorca.

Pharmacies *(farmácias)* are open during normal shopping hours, but there is at least one – the *farmácia de guardia* – open all night in Palma and in the large resorts. In small towns, it may be difficult to find an after-hours pharmacy. A list of the particular pharmacy on rota duty is (theoretically at least) posted in chemists' windows. Spanish pharmacists are highly trained and generally speak at least some English; they can dispense drugs over the counter that would often need a prescription elsewhere.

In Palma, the Farmácia March at Avinguda Joan Miró 186 (tel: 971 402 133) is open 24 hours a day, 365 days a year.

Emergency medical assistance can be obtained by dialling 112 or 061 (Ambulance service).

Major hospitals in Palma include: Son Espases, Carretera de Valldemossa (tel: 871 205 000(; and Hospital de la Creu Roja Espanyola, Carrer Pons i Gallarça 90 (tel: 971 751 445).

Where's the nearest (all-night) chemist? **¿Dónde está la farmácia (de guardia) más cercana?**
I need a doctor/dentist. **Necesito un médico/dentista**.
sunburn/sunstroke **quemadura del sol/una insolación**
an upset stomach **molestias de estómago**

L

LANGUAGE

The Balearics, including Mallorca, has two official languages: Castilian Spanish – the national language of Spain – and Catalan, spoken here in the form of a local dialect, Mallorquín; almost all islanders speak both with equal fluency.

Street and road signs appear only in Catalan. English and German are widely understood, especially in the resort areas.

> Do you speak English? **¿Habla usted inglés?**
> I don't speak Spanish. **No hablo español.**

LGBTQ+ TRAVELLERS

The Balearics are among the most hospitable places in Spain for LGBTQ+ travellers. Mallorca has a number of establishments, including hotels, bars, discos and restaurants that cater for the LGBTQ+ community or are LGBTQ-friendly. For information on the best places to go, you might consider contacting Ben Amics, Carrer Guillem Galmés 2, Palma (tel: 608 366 869; www.benamics.com).

M

MAPS

Detailed road maps of Mallorca are widely available from newsagents, tourist offices, petrol stations, souvenir shops and bookshops. They almost always have a more detailed inset map of Palma, the island's only city.

> Do you have a map of the city/island? **¿Tiene un plano de la ciudad/isla?**

MEDIA

In the main tourist areas, a scattering of English and German newspapers is sold on the day of publication. However, with the irresistible rise of the internet, the number of publications available, and the range of places that sell them, has plummeted. More positively, the *Majorca Daily Bulletin* (www.majorcadailybulletin.com), an English-language publication geared mainly to a British ex-pat readership, offers an informative round-up of island news and is a good online resource to find out about events. For Spanish speakers, the *Diario de Mallorca* (www.diariodemallorca.es) provides a comparable service.

Most hotels and bars have television, usually tuned to sports, and broadcasting in Castilian, Catalan (from Barcelona) and Mallorquín. Multiple cable channels (German, French, Sky, BBC, CNN, etc) are commonplace. Reception of the BBC World Service (www.bbc.co.uk) radio is usually good.

MONEY

Currency. Since 2002, Spain's currency has been the euro (€), which is divided into 100 cents. Bank notes are available in denominations of 5, 10, 20, 50, 100, 200 and 500 euros, and there are coins for 1 and 2 euros and for 1, 2, 5, 10, 20 and 50 cents. Note that the €500 is regarded with great suspicion – and many places will not accept them.

Currency exchange. You can exchange currency at banks (usually no commission charge) and *casas de cambio* (currency exchange stores) which stay open outside banking hours. Always take your passport as proof of identity. Check the rates carefully before handing over your money.

ATMs. The easiest way of obtaining cash, but check how much your bank will charge you for doing so. Some credit-card companies don't charge for withdrawing cash from ATMs abroad or for making other transactions.

Where's the nearest bank/currency exchange office? **¿Dónde está el banco más cercano/la oficina de cambio más cercana?**

I want to change some dollars/pounds. **Quiero cambiar dólares/ libres esterlina.**

Can I pay with this credit card? **¿Puedo pagar con esta tarjeta de crédito?**

O

OPENING HOURS

Most shops and offices are open from 9am to 1pm and again from 5pm until 8pm. Many museums and other tourist attractions maintain the same schedule, although increasingly the more popular ones are staying open all day. Large supermarkets and department stores usually stay open all day and some until 10pm. Banks generally open Mon–Fri 9am–2pm, and Sat 9am–1pm in winter only.

Restaurants serve lunch 1–3.30pm. In the evenings timing depends on the kind of customers they expect. Locals usually eat between 9.30 and 11pm. Places catering for foreigners may function from 7pm, and many serve food throughout the afternoon.

P

POLICE

Dial 092 for municipal police and 091 for national police. The general emergency number is 112. The municipal police station in Palma is located at Carrer de Son Dameto 1.

POST OFFICES

Identified by yellow and white signs with a crown, post offices are for mail; you can't phone from them (www.correos.es). The postal system is mostly reliable and efficient. Special delivery is always a good idea if you want to make sure of a speedy delivery. Opening hours are usually Monday to Friday 9am–2pm.

The main post office in Palma is located on Carrer Constitució 5 (just off Passeig des Born), and is open Mon–Fri 8.30am–8.30pm. Stamps (*segells*) are also sold by tobacconists (*tabacs*) and by most shops selling postcards. Post boxes are unmissable – large and bright yellow, with 'Correos' written down the side.

Where is the (nearest) post office? **¿Dónde está la oficina de correos (más cercana)?**
A stamp for this letter/postcard, please. **Por favor, un sello para esta carta/tarjeta.**

PUBLIC HOLIDAYS

The following are official public holidays (excludes saints' days).

1 January **Año Nuevo** New Year's Day
6 January **Epifanía** Epiphany
20 January **San Sebastián** St Sebastian's Day
1 May **Día del Trabajo** Labour Day
15 August **Asunción** Assumption
12 October **Día de la Hispanidad** National Day
1 November **Todos los Santos** All Saints' Day
6 December **Día de la** Constitución Constitution Day
8 December **Inmaculada Concepción** Immaculate Conception
24 December Christmas Eve
25 December **Navidad** Christmas Day
26 December Boxing Day/St Stephen's Day

Movable dates:

Late March/April **Jueves Santo** Maundy Thursday
Late March/April **Viernes Santo** Good Friday
Late March/April **Lunes de Pascua** Easter Monday
Mid-June **Corpus Christi** Corpus Christi

R

RELIGION

Spain is a predominantly Catholic country, although the church is in steep decline. Worshippers do, however, prefer visitors to show respect when entering a church, which includes wearing appropriate clothing (no bare shoulders, chests or short shorts, for instance).

T

TELEPHONES

Spain's country code is 34. The local area code is 971 and must be dialled before all phone numbers, even for local calls.

Coin and card-operated telephone booths were once plentiful, but are now all but obsolete. To make an international call, dial 00, plus the country code and the phone number, omitting any initial zero.

If you are going to make lots of calls within Spain, it is worth buying a Spanish SIM card or new phone from a phone shop. Well-known networks are Movistar (www.movistar.es) and Vodafone (www.vodafone.es). If you are using your usual phone and SIM, check with your network provider before you go that you have international roaming and find out if you can buy bundles of minutes to use abroad. It is often cheaper to receive calls than to make them. Spanish mobile phones operate on GSM 900/1800 or 3G 2100.

EU citizens can use their phones in other EU countries without incurring additional roaming fees: there is no extra charge for using your minutes, texts or data while you are away. Since the UK left the EU, some companies have reinstated (extortionate) roaming charges, some have not; check the situation with your provider.

TIME DIFFERENCES

The Balearics keep the same time as mainland Spain, which is one hour ahead of GMT, so Spanish time is generally one hour ahead of London, the same as Paris and Johannesburg, and six hours ahead of New York; it is nine hours behind Sydney and eleven hours behind Auckland.

TIPPING

Tipping in Spain is not customary but, in some places, it is welcomed to leave something small. A service charge is sometimes included on restaurant bills *(servicio incluido)*. If not, it is usual to tip waiters 10 percent; you can leave a few coins, rounding up the bill, in a bar. Give porters, hotel cleaners and hair-dressers about €1–2. It is not expected to tip a taxi driver but for exceptional service, you can tip up to 10 percent.

TOILETS

There are many expressions for toilets in Spanish: *baños*, *servicios*, *lavabos*, *aseos*, *wc* and *bater*. The first three are the most commonly used. Toilet doors usually have a 'C' for *Caballeros* (men), an 'S' for *Señoras* (women). Public toilets exist in some large towns, but they are rare; many bars will allow you to use their facilities.

TOURIST INFORMATION OFFICES

Spanish National Tourist Office (SNTO). The compendious website compiled by the Spanish National Tourist Office (www.spain.info) provides an excellent introduction to the country; its myriad synopses – on everything from national parks to accommodation – are well written and succinct.

Tourist offices abroad

Canada: 2 Bloor Street West, Suite 3402, Toronto, Ontario, M4W 3E2, tel: 416-961 3131.

UK: 2nd Floor, Heron House, 10 Dean Farrar St, SW1H 0DX, London, tel: 020 7317 2011.

US: Chicago: 333 N Michigan Avenue, Suite 2800 IL. 60601, Chicago, tel: 312-642 1992; Los Angeles: 8383 Wilshire Boulevard, Suite 960, Beverly Hills, CA 90211, tel: 323-658 7195; Suite 5300 New York: 60 East 42nd Street, New York, NY 10165–0039, tel: 212-265 8822; Miami: 2655 Le Jeune Rd (Gables International Plaza), Suite 605, Coral Gables FL 33134 Miami, tel: 305- 774 9643.

Tourist offices in Mallorca

Palma: Airport, tel: 971 789 556. For tourist information on the whole island, Plaça de la Reina 2, tel: 971 173 990. Municipal Tourist Offices (for information on Palma only): Plaça d'Espanya, tel: 902 102 365.

Sóller: Plaça d'Espanya s/n, tel: 971 638 008.

Pollença: Carrer de Guillem Cifre de Colonya 4, tel: 971 535 077.

TRANSPORT

Mallorca has a reliable and comprehensive transport system, its buses and trains serving almost all the island's towns and villages. You can get both bus and train timetables from the information office in Palma's Estació Intermodal (to the right of the entrance) or online at www.tib.org.

Bus. Buses (*autobús*) are clean, efficient and easy to use, and drivers are generally helpful. Destinations are marked on the front of the bus, and each town has its own bus station or terminal. In Palma, buses begin their journeys in the Estació Intermodal, the combined bus and railway station across the road from Plaça d'Espanya. Long-distance buses are coordinated by Transports de les Illes Balears (www.tib.org), and Palma services by Empresa Municipal de Transports (www.emtpalma.cat). There is a set fare for city journeys, and you buy your ticket on the bus. There is also the hop-on, hop-off tourist bus.

Train. Mallorca has three narrow-gauge train (*tren*) lines. All of them depart and end at Palma's Estació Intermodal on Plaça d'Espanya. The first one connects Palma with Inca, the second one to Sa Pobla, the third to Manacor. For more information, visit the Transports de le Illes Balears website: www.tib.org.

Ferries. Car ferries run a few times a day between Port d'Alcúdia and Ciutadella in Menorca, and take around two hours (Baleària, www.balearia.com). Transmediterránea (www.transmediterranea.es) has a weekly sailing from Palma to Mahón. Baleària also runs daily services from Palma to Ibiza, which take two hours. Note that you cannot take a car hire from one Balearic island to another.

Taxi. Taxi rates are metered and controlled by municipal diktat. In Palma, Radio Taxi: tel: 971 755 440; Taxi Palma Radio: tel: 971 401 414/971 702 424. In Sóller, tel: 971 638 484; in Pollença, tel: 971 866 213. In Cala Ratjada, tel: 971 819 090. Fares are reasonable, if not inexpensive: the fare for the 12km journey from the airport to the centre of Palma is, for example, €20; Søller to Pollença (55km) €90; there are small surcharges for excess baggage and late-night journeys. Always ask for a quote before you get in the car.

How much is it to the centre of town? **¿Cuanto es para ir al centro?**

V

VISAS AND ENTRY REQUIREMENTS (See also Embassies)

At time of writing, citizens of the EU/EEA, plus citizens of the UK, Australia, New Zealand, Canada and the USA, do not need a visa to enter Spain if staying for three months or less, but they do need a current passport. For non-EU citizens, this will almost certainly be modified in the next year or so when the EU introduces the ETIAS Visa Waiver – an online form, which must be completed before arrival and is an accompaniment to a passport. It is envisaged that, once the form is approved, the ETIAS Visa Waiver will be valid for multiple visits to Spain of up to three months each, over a three-year period. Travellers from South Africa currently need a passport and a tourist visa for visits of under three months; these visas must be obtained before departure and are available online from the Spanish embassy (see page 121). For stays of longer than three months, there are few hindrances for EU/EEA residents, but everyone else needs a mix of visas and permits. In all cases, consult your Spanish embassy at home before departure. For UK citizens, check www.gov.uk.

W

WEBSITES

www.illesbalears.travel Official tourist site for the Balearic Islands.

www.angloinfo.com/balearics Business directory, classifieds and what's on.

www.balearsnatura.com Detailed lowdown on all the island's natural parks.

https://caminsdepedra.conselldemallorca.cat Introduction to Mallorca's main long-distance hiking route, the *ruta de pedra en sec* (dry-stone route) – the GR221.

www.majorcadailybulletin.com A lively mix of news and gossip.

www.infomallorca.net Outstanding government-run tourism website.

www.spain.info Official website of the Spanish National Tourist Office (SNTO), with details on everything from national parks to accommodation.

www.tib.org Excellent site carrying all the details of public transport systems on Mallorca.

WHERE TO STAY

There is a wide range of accommodation available on Mallorca, anything and everything from luxury hotels to small, family-run *hostales*, as well as huge, impersonal, but usually very efficient, modern hotels in the bigger resorts, where much of the accommodation is block-booked by tour companies. There is also a growing crop of small, stylish hotels dotted across inland towns, many of which are delightful. Some hotels close for a few months in winter, so finding inexpensive off-season accommodation isn't always easy. For details on rural *(agroturisme)* holidays and staying in hermitages and sanctuaries, contact the tourism board.

In 2016, a sustainable tourism tax was introduced, commonly known as the "tourist tax". In 2019, it was increased, so now in addition to IVA (VAT), each visitor over the age of 16 will pay €4, €3, €2 or €1 per night, depending on the type of accommodation; there's a 50 percent reduction for stays over eight nights.

Most hotel rates include breakfast and tax, but it is not standard, so it is wise to check. Each accommodation reviewed in this Guide is accompanied by a price category, based on the cost of a standard double room in high season. Hotel rates include breakfast and tax, but it is not always standard, so it is wise to check before booking.

€€€€	**over 250 euros**
€€€	**150–250 euros**
€€	**100–150 euros**
€	**below 100 euros**

PALMA

Almudaina €€€ *Avinguda Jaume III 9, tel: 971 727 340*; www.hotelalmudaina. com. Established in 1972, the *Almudaina* is comfortable and moderately priced, with obliging staff. It is set on Palma's main shopping artery, and rooms on upper floors and the rooftop area have magnificent views over the city and the sea.

Born €€€ *Carrer Sant Jaume 3, tel: 971 712 942*; www.hotelborn.com. In a restored sixteenth-century mansion just off Plaça Rei Joan Carles II, this hotel is one of Palma's best bargains. With a grand central staircase and beautiful courtyard beneath Renaissance-style arches, it brims with atmosphere. Though not in the luxury league, the rooms are charming and very comfortable. Substantial breakfast, served in the courtyard. Advance reservations are essential; this place is popular.

Convent de la Missió €€€€ *Carrer de la Missió 7A, tel: 971 227 347*; www.conventdelamissio.com. This stylish hotel, in a converted seventeenth-century convent in the old part of town, has light, airy rooms, a roof terrace, solarium and steam rooms, plus an excellent Michelin-starred restaurant, *Marc Fosh*.

Hostal Apuntadores € *Carrer Apuntadors 8*; www.apuntadoreshostal.com. A long-established hostal with simple, straightforward rooms – and a good reputation – in a centrally located old house just off Passeig d'es Born. Some rooms are en suite (a few euros extra), others have an external bathroom, but light sleepers should bag a room at the back as c/Apuntadors can get very noisy at night.

Hotel H M Jaime III €€ *Passeig Mallorca 14*; www.hmjaimeiii.com. Four-star hotel with smart modern rooms kitted out in crisp, minimalist style. The public areas are a little overdone – there's usually a large and rather strange art installation of some description in the foyer – but that's hardly a major drawback. The guest rooms at the front, overlooking the Passeig Mallorca, have the advantage of a private balcony, but try to keep to the upper floors away from the noise of the city traffic.

Palacio Ca Sa Galesa €€€€ *Carrer Miramar 8, tel: 971 715 400*; www.palaciocasagalesa.com. Housed in a grand, meticulously restored seventeenth-century palace, this tiny twelve-room hotel is peppered with antiques, has a courtyard with fountain, and an indoor pool. Wheelchair access.

Palau Sa Font €€€ *Calle Apuntadores 38, tel: 971 712 277*; www.palausafont.com. A delightful hotel in a sixteenth-century episcopal palace, with nineteen individually decorated rooms – those at the back are quieter, but this is the peaceful end of a busy street.

Petit Palace Hotel Tres €€€€ *Carrer Apuntadores 3, tel: 971 717 333*; www.hoteltres.com. Hipster-tripster hotel with a lovely old courtyard, a sleek bar, ultra-smart bathrooms and a rooftop terrace with a splash pool.

San Lorenzo €€€ *Carrer San Lorenzo 14, tel: 971 728 200*; www.hotelsanlorenzo.com. This enchanting nine-room hotel is always booked up well in advance. Excellent-value guest rooms are all individually decorated; each has its own balcony, some open onto the tranquil little garden. There's a small swimming pool too.

THE WESTERN CORNER
Banyalbufar

Sa Baronia € *c/Baronia 16, tel: 971 618 146*; www.hbaronia.com. This endearingly simple hotel, tucked into the folds of terraced hills, partly inhabits an ancient fortified house. The rooms are a tad spartan, but adequate; all have sea-facing terraces.

Mar i Vent €€ *Carrer Major 49, tel: 971 618 000*; www.hotelmarivent.com. Attractive family-owned hotel poised atop a cliff, with a restaurant, terrace, garden, tennis court and swimming pool. It has a clutch of comfortable rooms and stunning sea views. A path leads down to two quiet coves.

Estellencs

Finca S'Olivar €€–€€€ *Carretera C-710 Km 93.5, tel: 971 618 593*; www.fincaolivar.org. Gorgeous *agroturisme* cradled in the belly of a six-hectare (15-acre) private valley, with wonderful views over the coast. The self-catering accommodation is spread across two traditional stone houses and two cottages. The icing on the cake: an idyllic infinity pool with terrace.

Illetes

Bon Sol €€€–€€€€ *Passeig de Illetes 30, tel: 971 402 111*; www.hotelbonsol.es. A family-run, antique-filled hotel on multiple levels, cascading down pine-shaded cliffs to its own beach. There's a restaurant, sun terraces, gym and spa.

Portals Nous

Bendinat €€€€ *Carrer Andres Ferret Sobral 1, tel: 971 675 725*; www.hotel-bendinat.es. A handsome hacienda-style hotel hugging a small, rocky cove. There are smart guest rooms with balconies and bungalows sheltered among terraced gardens. It's situated close to seven golf courses.

Port d'Andratx

Brismar €€ *Almirante Riera Alemany 6, tel: 971 671 600*; www.hotelbrismar.com. This comfortable, long-established seafront hotel is a bargain given the coveted location. Ask for a room with a harbour view, though these are the noisiest. Wheelchair access. In summer, three nights minimum stay.

THE WEST COAST
Deià

Belmond La Residencia €€€€ *Son Canals s/n, Deià, tel: 971 639 011*; www.belmond.com/la-residencia-mallorca. Luxurious hotel, owned by Belmond Hotels, located in two immaculately modernized sixteenth-century manor houses. A chic, wealthy international clientele enjoys a spa and health centre, beautiful swimming pools, tennis courts, and *El Olivo*, one of the island's finest restaurants.

Hostal Villa Verde €€ *Carrer Ramón Llull 19, Deià, tel: 971 639 037*; www.hostalvillaverde.es. A simple, friendly little place with a family atmosphere, situated on the way up to the church, with an inviting garden and terrace.

S'Hotel d'es Puig €€€ *Carrer d'es Puig 4, Deià, tel: 971 639 409*; www.hotel-despuig.com. Hidden down the cobbled streets of Deià, this delightful little hotel has a huddle of bright and airy rooms, a serve-yourself bar and a relaxed, friendly atmosphere. Also has four apartments to let in a nearby house, and tenants can use the hotel pool.

Miramar €€ *Carrer Ca'n Oliver s/n, Deià, tel: 971 639 084*; www.pensionmira-mardeia.com. Set above the main road up a narrow byroad, this lovely *hos-*

tal has a cavernous entrance hall and rooms with and without bathrooms. Breakfast is served on the terrace.

Es Molí €€€€ *Carretera Valldemossa–Deià s/n, Deià, tel: 971 639 000*; www. esmoli.com. Elegant hotel in a nineteenth-century manor house just outside Deià, with unrivalled views of the village and the sea. The pool is spring-fed, and the hotel is set among 1.5 hectares (4 acres) of lush gardens. The service is splendid. Breakfast is served outside on the terrace.

Port de Sóller

Aimia €€ *c/Santa Maria del Camí 1 tel: 971 631 200*; www.aimiahotel.com. In a low modern block, this perfectly maintained four-star hotel has the most comfortable of guest rooms, each with the unmistakeable flourishes of a designer's touch. There's a spa, gym and a garden pool – and it's all reassuringly smart and relaxing.

Jumeirah Port Sóller Hotel & Spa €€€€ *Carrer Belgica s/n, tel: 971 637 888*; www.jumeirah.com. This five-star beauty has every luxury you might expect: clifftop views, three gourmet restaurants, two bars, three pools and a spa.

Es Port €€€ *Antonio Montis s/n, Port de Sóller, tel: 971 631 650*; www.hoteles-port.com. The most attractive hotel in the port, with lovely gardens, sun terraces and great views. Steps from the beach, this seventeenth-century manor house has wood-beamed ceilings and attractive rooms. Two good restaurants, plus a string of heated pools; thalassotherapy is available for guests.

Sóller

S'Ardeviu €€€ *Carrer Vives 14, tel: 971 638 326*; www.hotelsardeviu.com. A comfortable and attractive hotel, with just seven guest rooms and a pretty garden. It's a peaceful spot in a narrow street, though it's close to the vibrant Plaça Major.

Ca n'Aí Hotel Rural €€€€ *Camí Son Sales 50 (Cta Sóller–Deià), Sóller, tel: 971 632 494*; www.canai.com. Family-run for generations, this restored stone manor house is set in canal-threaded grounds, surrounded by orange and lemon groves. There's a swimming pool shaded by palm trees, and thirty suites with terraces.

El Guía €€ *Carrer Castanyer 2 Sóller, tel: 971 630 227*; www.hotelelguia.com. Opened in 1880, this traditional hotel offers excellent value. It was fully renovated in 2017, and is footsteps from the railway station. Attractive courtyard, and an in-house restaurant serving typical Mallorcan dishes.

Valldemossa

Ca's Papa €€ *c/Jovellanos 8, tel: 971 612 808*; www.hotelcaspapa.com. Charming independent hotel in a great location, just metres from the monastery, in a brightly painted old stone-terraced house. Just thirteen cosily decorated rooms – no chain lookalikes here.

Hotel Valldemossa €€€€ *Carretera Vieja de Valldemossa s/n, tel: 971 612 626*; www.valldemossahotel.com. On the outskirts of town, ringed by orange and olive groves, this luxurious hotel is set in two nineteenth-century mansions. Guest rooms are peppered with antiques and artworks.

THE NORTH
Alcúdia

Ca'n Simó Petit Hotel €€ *Carrer Sant Jaume 1, tel: 971 515 260*; www.cancalcohotels.com. Bare stone walls, exposed beams and an attractive courtyard give this small hotel, in a converted nineteenth-century townhouse, its character. Smart bathrooms, attractive rooms and an excellent restaurant.

Sant Jaume €€ *Carrer Sant Jaume 6, tel: 971 549 419*; www.hotelsantjaume. com. Close to the city walls, this nineteenth-century landowners' mansion is furnished in keeping with the period. There are a six individually designed rooms, a pretty patio with a fountain, and an open fire to warm cool evenings.

Cala Sant Vicenç

Cala Sant Vicenç €€€ *Carrer Maressers 2, tel: 971 530 250*; www.hotelcala. com. Beautifully renovated adults-only property in this stunning little bay. Relaxed but extremely efficient. The *Lavanda* restaurant is recommended. Wheelchair access.

Hoposa Niu €€€ *Carrer Cala Barques 5, tel: 971 530 512*; www.hoposa.es. This well-situated modern hotel overlooks the lovely cove of Cala Sant Vicenç. Facilities include terraces, bar and a competent restaurant specializing in fish and lobster. The rooftop swimming pool looks out over the sea. Reserve well in advance.

Pollença

Ermita de Nostra Senyora del Puig de Maria € *2km south of town (see page 135), tel: 971 18 41 32*. At this hilltop monastery, the original monks' quarters have been renovated to provide simple, unassuming guest rooms with shared facilities. To be sure of a room, book ahead, but be warned that it can get cold and windy at night, even in the summer months. There's a refectory on site, but the food is only average. Open all year. Singles, doubles and triples are all available.

L'Hostal €€ *Carrer Mercat 18, tel: 971 535 002*; www.pollensahotels.com. Run by the owners behind the popular *Juma* (below), this *hotel d'interior* is housed in a traditional townhouse, but the large rooms are modern and minimalist, with pale wood and bright colours. Shares a reception with sister hotel *Juma*.

Juma €€ *Plaça Major 9, tel: 971 535 002*; www.pollensahotels.com. This small, smart seven-room hotel, occupying a *Moderniste* building right on Pollença's picturesque plaza, has been pleasing loyal guests since 1905. The clutch of guest rooms are comfortable and airy, and there's a pleasant restaurant on the ground floor.

Son Sant Jordi €€€ *Calle Sant Jordi 29, tel: 971 530 389*; www.sonsantjordi. com. Located in the heart of Pollença, this appealing hotel offers period-style rooms in a string of old and attractively modernized townhouses. There's a restaurant, spa and swimming pool.

Port de Pollença

Hoposa Hotel Daina €€€ *c/Atilio Boveri 2*, www.hoposa.es. Straightforward tower-block hotel with seventy-odd rooms and an excellent seashore location beside Passeig Anglada Camarasa. The public areas are slick and modern, as are the bedrooms. There's an outside swimming pool too.

Hotel Bahia €€€ *Paseo Voramar s/n, tel: 971 866 562*; www.hoposa.es. A seaside bolthole in a nineteenth-century summer home, with an inviting terrace.

Miramar €€€ *Passeig Anglada Camarasa 39, tel: 971 866 400*; www.hotel-miramar.net. A long-established beachfront hotel with a terrace overlooking the bay and Cap de Formentor. Guest rooms open onto balconies but not all of them face the beach, so check when you book.

Pension Bellavista € *c/Monges 14, tel: 971 86 46 00*; www.pensionbellavista. com. Funkiest place in town, with a laidback vibe and a handful of straightforward but comfortable en-suite rooms; set a brief walk from the seafront in a 1930s house. Breakfasts are vegetarian extravaganzas.

Sis Pins €€ *Passeig Anglada Camarasa 77, tel: 971 867 050*; www.hotelsispins. com. This pretty green-shuttered hotel with friendly staff is right on the beach. The bad news is that many rooms, especially those with sea-view balconies, are booked by tour operators or repeat customers. Well worth a try, though.

THE CENTRAL PLAIN

Inca

Virrey €€€ *Carretera Inca-Sencelles Km 2.4, tel: 971 881 018*; www.virreyhotel.com. This majestic mansion has been reimagined as a chic boutique hotel with spectacular guest rooms, a Mallorcan restaurant and an outdoor pool.

Sineu

Sa Bassa Rotja €€€€ *Finca Son Orell, Cami de Sa Pedrera s/n, Porreres, tel: 971 168 225*; www.sabassarotja.com. A grand country mansion with sports facilities and a restaurant showcasing local ingredients. Ideal for a relaxing break.

Son Bernadinet €€€ *Carretera Campos–Porreres Km 5.9, tel: 971 650 694*; www. son-bernadinet.com. An inviting manor house ringed by almond orchards, with its own vegetable gardens, and a log fire to warm you in winter. It feels miles from anywhere, but it's only fifteen minutes' drive to the nearest beach.

THE EAST AND SOUTHEAST

Artà

Casal d'Artà €€ *Carrer Rafael Blanes 19, tel: 971 829 163*; www.casaldarta.de. A small family-run hotel in the centre of town, gazing out over a leafy square. Some *Moderniste* features, including swathes of stained glass. Some guest rooms have four-poster beds, and there's a lovely roof terrace for catching the last of the day's rays.

Cala d'Or

Cala d'Or €€€ *Avinguda Bélgica 49, tel: 971 657 249*; www.hotelcalador.com. Peaking out from a pine grove, this smart hotel overlooks a semi-private cove. Friendly staff, and all the facilities you would expect. Excellent value for money.

Cala Figuera

Villa Sirena €€ *Carrer Virgen del Carmen 37, tel: 971 645 303,* www.hotelvil-lasirena.com. A good-value modern hotel right by the sea, at the edge of this pretty village. Closed Nov–March.

Cala Ratjada

Cala Ratjada € *Carrer Llevamans 2, tel: 971 563 202,* www.hostalcalaratjada. com. A pleasant one-star *hostal* right by the port, with en-suite rooms. Good budget choice; book in advance.

Porto Colom

Hostal Porto Colom €€ *Carrer Cristófol Colom 5, tel: 971 825 323,* www. hostalportocolom.com. Situated right by the port, this modern hotel in an ochre-coloured abode offers a clutch of comfortable guest rooms. There's a Mediterranean restaurant and a cocktail bar with live music.

INDEX

THE **MINI** ROUGH GUIDE TO
MALLORCA

First edition 2023

Editor: Joanna Reeves
Author: Phil Lee
Picture Editor: Tom Smyth
Cartography Update: Katie Bennett
Layout: Grzegorz Madejak
Head of DTP and Pre-Press: Katie Bennett
Head of Publishing: Kate Drynan
Photography Credits: Adobe Stock 94; Bar
Cristal 6T; Bigstock 65; Fotolia 19; Glyn Genin/Apa
Publications 102; Greg Gladman/Apa Publications
5M, 5M, 5M, 7T, 11, 13, 14, 18, 23, 26, 31, 32, 33, 35, 36,
38, 39, 41, 42, 44, 48, 49, 53, 57, 59, 60, 63, 66, 71, 73,
74, 77, 78, 80, 84, 85, 89, 96, 105; iStock 4TL, 5T, 5T, 5T
6B, 54, 69, 82, 86, 91, 100; Orient Express 7B; Public
domain 20; Shutterstock 1, 4ML, 4ML, 5M, 17, 28, 29,
46, 51, 93, 98, 104
Cover Credits: Lighthouse of Cap de Formentor
Shutterstock

Distribution

UK, Ireland and Europe: Apa Publications (UK)
Ltd; sales@roughguides.com
United States and Canada: Ingram Publisher
Services; ips@ingramcontent.com
Australia and New Zealand: Booktopia;
retailer@booktopia.com.au
Worldwide: Apa Publications (UK) Ltd;
sales@roughguides.com

**Special Sales, Content Licensing
and CoPublishing**
Rough Guides can be purchased in bulk quantities
at discounted prices. We can create special editions,
personalised jackets and corporate imprints
tailored to your needs. sales@roughguides.com;
http://roughguides.com

Printed in China

This book was produced using **Typefi** automated
publishing software.

Contact us
Every effort has been made to provide accurate
information in this publication, but changes
are inevitable. The publisher cannot be held
responsible for any resulting loss, inconvenience
or injury sustained by any traveller as a result of
information or advice contained in the guide.
We would appreciate it if readers would call our
attention to any errors or outdated information,
or if you feel we've left something out. Please
send your comments with the subject line "Rough
Guide Mini Rough Guide Mini Mallorca Update" to
mail@uk.roughguides.com.